FOLLOWING *Christ* AND FISHING *for Men*

CLARENCE SEXTON

CROWN
PUBLICATIONS
Royal Reading

FOLLOWING *Christ* AND FISHING *FOR Men*

CLARENCE SEXTON

FIRST EDITION
COPYRIGHT
NOVEMBER 2002

CROWN
PUBLICATIONS
Royal Reading

1700 BEAVER CREEK DRIVE
POWELL, TENNESSEE ❖ 37849
1-877 AT CROWN
www.FaithfortheFamily.com

FOLLOWING CHRIST AND FISHING FOR MEN

Formerly *Won by One*, Sword of the Lord, 1978

Copyright © 2002

Crown Publications

Powell, Tennessee 37849

ISBN: 1-58981-123-2

Layout and design by Stephen Troell & Joshua Tangeman

Printed in the United States of America

Dedication

This book is dedicated to the wonderful people of the Temple Baptist Church who have followed these biblical principles in the matter of witnessing to the lost.

I also deeply appreciate our dedicated staff for exemplifying the truth of *Following Christ and Fishing for Men.*

Clarence Sexton
Acts 5:42

Introduction

R.A. Torrey once said, "My one ambition in life is to win as many souls as I possibly can. It is the most worthwhile thing in life."

In the pages to follow, you will find a biblical approach to personal evangelism. This book is meant to be more than a series of lessons on personal soul winning. The purpose of this book is to stir Christians to follow Christ and fish for men.

The Lord Jesus Christ has the power to save and transform lives, and He has chosen to use human instruments to get the glorious gospel message to dying men.

It is the responsibility of every Christian to go in the power of the Holy Spirit to the lost, give them a clear presentation of the gospel, and bring them to the place of receiving or rejecting the Lord Jesus Christ as their personal Savior.

Every Christian is either a road or a roadblock in the carrying out of this Great Commission. Allow the Lord to use you to win souls!

Clarence Sexton

Acts 5:42

Contents

"And he saith unto them, Follow me, and I will make you fishers of men. And they straightway left their nets, and followed him."

Matthew 4:19-20

FOLLOWING CHRIST AND FISHING FOR MEN

 any churches are changing. All over the world, churches have fallen into the "success syndrome." The measure of whether or not they are getting the job done has become little more than keeping score. I am grateful to God for the wonderful number of people who attend our church, the generous giving on the part of God's people, and for the many who come to know Christ as Savior; but the measure of our ministry must always be in our likeness to Christ.

In many churches the pastor no longer has a study; he only has an office. The pastor is no longer a shepherd; he must be a CEO. Many pastors are no longer preachers; they are heads of the leadership teams. We have taken the terms of the world and applied them to the things of God.

Believers in the Lord Jesus would revolt if I tried to teach that one could become a Christian without Christ. I would have a real mutiny on my hands, and rightly so, if I tried to teach that one could become a Christian without Christ.

> *The measure of our ministry must always be in our likeness to Christ.*

There is no difference between attempting to teach someone to become a Christian without Christ and attempting to live the Christian life without Christ. It cannot be done.

If we are going to have spiritual ends, we must have spiritual means. If we are going to achieve biblical goals, we must do it by spiritual and scriptural means. This is the truth to consider as we deal with this passage of Scripture about our Lord Jesus in Matthew 4:12-20,

> *Now when Jesus had heard that John was cast into prison, he departed into Galilee; and leaving Nazareth, he came and dwelt in Capernaum, which is upon the sea coast, in the borders of Zabulon and Nephthalim: that it might be fulfilled which was spoken by Esaias the prophet, saying, The land of Zabulon, and the land of Nephthalim, by the way of the sea, beyond Jordan, Galilee of the Gentiles; the people which sat in darkness saw great light; and to them which sat in the region and shadow of death light is sprung up. From that time Jesus began to preach, and to say, Repent: for the kingdom of heaven is at hand. And Jesus, walking by the sea of Galilee, saw two brethren, Simon called Peter, and Andrew his brother, casting a net into the sea: for they were fishers. And he saith unto them, Follow me, and I will make you fishers of men. And they straightway left their nets, and followed him.*

Make special note of the expression in the nineteenth verse, *"Follow me, and I will make you fishers of men."* The believer is to follow Christ and fish for men.

There are no self-made spiritual men. Notice in the heart of this verse, the Lord says, *"I will make you."* We do not make ourselves. He makes us. The Lord Jesus Christ said, *"Follow me, and I will make you fishers of men."* Following Christ and fishing for men is for every Christian.

My family and I spent eight years in the greater New York City area as I served as pastor of the Madison Avenue Baptist Church in Paterson, New Jersey. Shortly after I arrived, one of the members of the church died and I was asked to conduct the funeral. I had gotten acquainted with the particular person who had died, but I did not know much about the area where he lived.

I went to conduct the funeral service at a funeral home in a township called Hawthorne, New Jersey. After the funeral service was concluded, I returned to my car, and we prepared to make our way to the cemetery in Paterson, New Jersey.

In Hawthorne, one of the Hawthorne Township police officers was assigned to lead the funeral procession and asked me to pull my car behind his and follow him. I took my place behind the police car with the hearse behind me. We started out on our journey to the cemetery in Paterson.

Having been in the area for only a short time, I did not know much about the streets, and I had no idea how to find my way to the cemetery. When we got to the township border of Hawthorne, the police officer left the procession and left me in front of the funeral procession. I had no idea where I was going. To make bad matters worse, I looked into my rearview mirror and there was no hearse, no family, and no one else behind me.

There I was supposedly leading a family and a hearse to a graveyard for a burial, and there was no funeral procession behind me. I was lost. The other cars had made a turn somewhere, and I did not know where they were.

I had been driving at a slow pace because of the funeral procession, so I knew I had to pick up speed. I stopped at a gasoline station and asked for directions to the cemetery. I followed the directions and pulled up at the gate of the cemetery just as the hearse and the other cars were arriving. I said to the funeral director after the graveside service was conducted, "I got lost." He said, "I thought you had something to care for and you'd catch up with us later."

I was sincere about the idea that I wanted to get to the right place. I knew that I had a responsibility I wanted to fulfill. I was very much aware of that, but I had no one to follow. I needed someone to follow.

There are many Christians in our churches who know that they are here on earth to tell others of the Savior, but the problem is they are not following the leadership of the Lord Jesus.

GOD WANTS EVERYONE TO BE SAVED

The Bible says in II Peter 3:9 that the Lord is *"not willing that any should perish, but that all should come to repentance."* God wants everyone to be saved. He wants you to become a Christian. He wants you to ask Him to forgive your sin and by faith trust the Lord Jesus Christ as your personal Savior.

GOD USES PEOPLE TO DO HIS WORK

A second thing we must realize is that God uses people to do His work. This is an amazing truth. The Lord uses human instruments to do His work.

EVERY ONE OF GOD'S CHILDREN IS COMMANDED TO LIVE A HOLY LIFE

A third thing is that every one of God's children is commanded to live a holy life. There are no options here. There is no middle ground. If you are one of God's children, you are commanded of God to live a holy life. The Bible says, *"Be ye holy; for I am holy"* (I Peter 1:16).

THE HOLY SPIRIT GIVES US POWER TO LIVE A HOLY LIFE

A fourth thing is that the Holy Spirit of God gives us power to live this holy life. We cannot live the Christian life in our own strength. The Christian life cannot be lived apart from Christ and the power of the indwelling Holy Spirit. You could no sooner become a Christian without Christ than live the Christian life without the power of the Holy Spirit. If you are trying to live the Christian life apart from the power of the Holy Spirit, it cannot be done and it will not be done.

GOD DOES HIS WORK IN THIS WORLD THROUGH THE LOCAL CHURCH

We must never forget that God does His work in this world through the local church. The best thing you can do as a Christian is to get involved in what your church is doing for the Lord. Find your place of service there. Do not try to get your church to cater to you. Find your place of service to God in your church. Put your whole heart into the ministry of your local church and serve God there.

In our Bible passage, we find the Lord Jesus Christ walking along the Sea of Galilee. He came to men who had already placed their faith in Him and had continued in their fishing business. He said to these men, *"Follow me, and I will make you fishers of men."* The Bible says in the twentieth verse, *"And they straightway left their nets, and followed him."* It is wonderful to be sensitive to the voice of God and to recognize God's voice as He speaks to us. We are to be obedient to Him. Delay is disobedience.

The Christian is to be sensitive to the leadership of the Lord and be willing to do whatever He desires. The Lord will direct those who are ready to obey. The moment I know clearly what God wants, I should delight in doing His will.

THE PRINCIPLE
EVERYTHING WE DO WITH AND FOR MEN MUST BE PRECEDED BY OUR TIME WITH GOD

Many have placed an emphasis on "follow up" to the neglect of the *"follow Me"* program. The Lord Jesus said, "Follow Me, then fish for men." The principle is very clear. Everything we do with and for men must be preceded by our time with God. The first call on our lives is a call to be *"with him"* (Mark 3:14).

If it is my responsibility to come to the pulpit and preach, I cannot preach as a pastor should preach unless I have first been with Christ. This principle is for every area of the Christian life.

If you are a mother, you are to minister to those children and care for those children. You cannot do for those children what you should do without following Christ.

As a Christian wife, you cannot be the right kind of wife to your husband without following Christ. No matter how much you know about being a wife, how good a cook you may be, how good a housekeeper you may be, it is impossible for you to be the Christian wife God wants you to be to your husband without spending time with God.

You may be the loveliest lady anyone has ever seen. You may be the most industrious woman anyone has ever met. You may be the neatest, most hard-working woman anyone has ever known. But there is something great missing in your life if this principle is not in practice—following Christ, then fishing for men. It must be Christ, then people. This same principle holds true for the husband. He must be a follower of Christ.

If you direct the choir in your church, you cannot direct the choir without spending time with the Lord and following Him. If you sing solos in your church services, it is Christ first, then singing. If you play an instrument in your church, it is Christ first, then playing the instrument.

The principle here applies to all of life. If you are a Christian businessman and you have employees, you cannot do what you should do as an employer without following Christ. There is no way the manward part can be cared for properly without caring for the Godward.

So many people think this is only for people in the ministry. Whatever sphere you operate in, it is the same principle for all Christians. It is following Christ, then fishing for men.

What is our great error? We rush and search for shortcuts. We do everything we can to eliminate the need for God so we can run ahead and do what we know we can do on our own.

The worst thing that happens to us is not that we fail. Our greatest failures take place as we succeed in areas that are not God's will and are not true to the clear teaching of God's Word. We build the business without spending time with God. We grow a church without spending time with God. We get a family to obey without spending time with God. We get the work done without spending time with God.

The Lord will speak to those who are ready to obey.

The worst thing about this is not that we fail; the worst thing is if we succeed having left Christ out. If we fail, we quickly learn that something is wrong; but when we succeed, it may take years, if ever, to get out of the "success syndrome" thinking, "I can do it the shortcut way without being the Christian God requires me to be."

There is such an important principle here. The Lord Jesus said, *"Follow me, and I will make you fishers of men."* What a powerful principle!

What is it God has for me? It is the same thing He has for you if you are a Christian. God wants you to worship Him, to abide in Him, to spend time with Him so that whatever you are called on to do can be done in a way that pleases Him and glorifies Him and brings the greatest satisfaction to your life.

All of us who are Christians and have lived a while have realized that when we do things without this order God has established, the work can grow and things can be accomplished, but the bigger it gets and the longer we work at it, the more exhausted we become and the less fulfilling it is. Finally we wonder, "What is wrong? I'm doing the right things. We are getting things done. We have some measure of success." God has designed the entire Christian life so that there is no deep satisfaction of the soul when God has not been placed where He should be placed in our lives. This is a convicting principle.

THE PRIORITY
FOLLOWING CHRIST AND FISHING FOR MEN

Notice in this simple passage the priority God establishes. The priority is following Christ and fishing for men. What does this mean? The Lord Jesus Himself said in Luke 19:10, *"For the Son of man is come to seek and to save that which was lost."*

The Lord Jesus found men who had been catching live fish and casting them aside to die. He called them to fish for men who were dead in trespasses and sins and would be made alive through the Lord Jesus Christ. This is the priority.

Most of us find something in God's work to do, other than fishing for men. So many go through the motions of Christianity but miss the priority God has given. People are lost without God and must be born again. Christians have a greater work to do than simply making the world a better place from which to go to hell.

In our churches, we get everything running and moving, and we think God is so very pleased with our activity; but what is the priority? He said, *"Follow me, and I will make you fishers of men."* If we have everything else right and this one thing wrong, then we have not succeeded everywhere else, we have failed everywhere else. It only appears that we have succeeded, but we have failed.

My dear friend Dr. Lee Roberson has said many times in my presence that most Christians do more witnessing to the lost in the first six months they are saved than they do in the rest of their lives. Why is that? Could it be that they are nearer the cross, closer to God, still thrilled about what God has done for them? Because of that, they are extremely excited about telling people about Christ.

> *God has designed the entire Christian life so that there is no deep satisfaction of the soul when He has not been placed where He should be placed in our lives.*

There is a priority here, "following Christ and fishing for men." What are we going to do? Let us pray, "Lord, help me to be willing to admit that my priority is wrong if my priority is not fishing for men."

THE PROGRESSION
AS WE FOLLOW CHRIST, HE MAKES US FISHERS OF MEN

As we follow Christ, we will fish for men. Again, the verse says, *"Follow me, and I will make you fishers of men."* Let us begin with *"fishers of men"* and work our way backward.

We are going to start at the end of this verse and work our way backward to see the progression. In the end of this verse, we are fishing for men; we are bringing people to Christ. As we work our way back, we move from *"fishers of men"* to *"I will make you."*

Christians have a greater work to do than simply making the world a better place from which to go to hell.

It is the Lord Jesus who transforms our lives. We were not fishers of men, we were fishers of fish; we were involved in other things. If we are *"fishers of men,"* it is because He has made us fishers of men. The Lord's promise says, "I will make you."

As we move to the head waters of this verse, we get to the place where we find that God says, *"Follow me."* What does all of this mean? If we are not fishing for men, it is because He did not make us fishers of men. If He did not make us fishers of men, it is because we are not following Him. If we are following Him, He is going to make us fishers of men. If we are not fishers of men, it is obvious that we are not following Him because if we are following Him, His passion will become our passion. His purpose will become our purpose. We will be fishers of men.

This is very difficult for me to admit, but when I am not conscious of souls, when I am not speaking to people about Christ as I should, there is only one reason for it. It is because Jesus Christ does not hold the place in my life that He should hold. If He truly holds the place He should hold in my life, then there is no doubt that He will make me a fisher of men. You can go after the lost without following Christ, but you cannot truly follow Christ without going after the lost.

I was just a teenager when I became a Christian. As I yielded my life to Christ, I wanted my brother to become a Christian, I wanted my two sisters to become Christians, and I wanted my mother to become a Christian. My father was already deceased, but I wanted to know if my father had died with or without Christ. It troubled me to think about it. My mother told me once near the end of my father's life, "Your father has gotten religion." That was her way of expressing an idea that he was talking about Christ and whistling songs about the Lord. A pastor told me, after I had been preaching for a number of years, that he had led my father to Christ shortly before he died.

What really matters in life is what we are most concerned about in death—whether or not people know Jesus Christ. If this is what matters most, then why is it that we do not give ourselves to what matters most? The reason is that there is something wrong in this principle, this priority, or this progression. We must go back upstream.

You do not become a witness, a fisher of men, by saying, "I'm going to be a fisher of men." It may last a while, but we must go back upstream and find that if we follow Christ, He will make us fishers of men.

My heart needs to be changed; my passion needs to be changed. What I do with my energy needs to be changed. I have already proven that I cannot change it. I will simply find something else to add to the long list of good things to do. It is only the Lord Jesus who can change the list and give me the right priority to be a fisher of men.

You can go after the lost without following Christ, but you cannot truly follow Christ without going after the lost.

The Lord said, *"Follow me, and I will make you fishers of men."* We are to follow Christ and fish for men. If we are having a people problem, the big problem is not the people problem, not the family problem, not the children problem, or the parental problem. If we are having people problems of any kind—and life is always going to be filled with people problems—the real problem is that we need to get where we should be with the Lord so we can deal with the people.

Our greatest failures take place as we succeed in areas that are not God's will and are not true to the clear teaching of God's Word.

Are you having a problem with the right priorities in your life? You say, "I'm just as busy as I can be, but I am seeing no one come to Christ." Let us deal with the real issue. The progression shows that we are not where we should be with the Lord or we would be doing what we should be doing for the Lord.

May the Lord deal with each of us. May He bring all of us to the place where we are willing to say, "Yes, Lord. Change me. Transform me. Work in my life." Let us follow Christ and fish for men.

We follow Christ by abiding in Him (John 15:4). We follow Christ as we rejoice in Him each day. He gives us His joy (John 15:11). He has called us to be with Him, and then He sends us forth to preach (Mark 3:14).

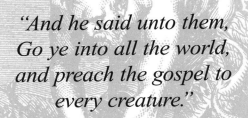

"And he said unto them, Go ye into all the world, and preach the gospel to every creature."

Mark 16:15

EVERY CHRISTIAN SHOULD SEEK TO WIN SOULS

alvation is of the Lord. Salvation is in the Person of Jesus Christ. We are to tell others of the gospel. The gospel is the Good News of Jesus Christ. In the very words of Scripture, the Bible declares,

Moreover, brethren, I declare unto you the gospel which I preached unto you, which also ye have received, and wherein ye stand; by which also ye are saved, if ye keep in memory what I preached unto you, unless ye have believed in vain. For I delivered unto you first of all that which I also received, how that Christ died for our sins according to the scriptures; and that he was buried, and that he rose again the third day according to the scriptures (I Corinthians 15:1-4).

The Lord Jesus Christ is not the plan of salvation; He is the way of salvation. We are to speak to people about the Person of Jesus Christ. They must know who He is and why they need Him. They must be told that they can know Him personally as their Savior.

It is the responsibility and privilege of every Christian to be a soul winner. It has been nearly two thousand years since our Lord left the church with the sacred responsibility of giving the gospel message to the world. Yet, so few who say they are His followers have obeyed Him. Let us take a fresh look at what He has commanded us to do.

THE COMMAND OF CHRIST

Our highest motive in the matter of soul winning must be one of love for our Savior, and out of this love comes a desire to obey His command.

THIS COMMAND HAS BEEN VERY CLEARLY GIVEN

As we go, He goes with us.

> *"Go ye therefore, and teach all nations, baptizing them in the name of the Father, and of the Son, and of the Holy Ghost: teaching them to observe all things whatsoever I have commanded you: and, lo, I am with you alway, even unto the end of the world. Amen."*
>
> Matthew 28:19-20

Miraculous things take place as God transforms lives through the power of the gospel. Read through the end of Mark chapter 16.

> *"And he said unto them, Go ye into all the world, and preach the gospel to every creature."*
>
> Mark 16:15

We must be witnesses before we can witness for Him. The noun comes before the verb.

> *"And said unto them, Thus it is written, and thus it behoved Christ to suffer, and to rise from the dead the third day: and that repentance and remission of sins should be preached in his name among all nations, beginning at Jerusalem. And ye are witnesses of these things."*
>
> Luke 24:46-48

He gives us authority to go.

> *"Then said Jesus to them again, Peace be unto you: as my Father hath sent me, even so send I you."*
>
> John 20:21

There is no place to stop. We must go to the uttermost part of the earth.

> *"But ye shall receive power, after that the Holy Ghost is come upon you: and ye shall be witnesses unto me both in Jerusalem, and in all Judæa, and in Samaria, and unto the uttermost part of the earth."*
>
> Acts 1:8

WHY OBEY HIM?

So often the need of mankind is considered to be the highest motive for personal evangelism; but according to the Word of God, our highest motive is the love of Christ. Paul said, *"For the love of Christ constraineth us"* (II Corinthians 5:14). Christ was motivated by love to go to Calvary, and it is His love that motivates us to witness for Him to others. Paul was compelled to go after souls because of the love of Christ.

Love for God or the Lostness of Sinners

The sinfulness of men keeps us from loving them as we should. If our motive for evangelism is our love for lost men, that motive will not be strong enough. The love of Christ is the only motive that will lead us on in the face of great disappointment or danger. When our motive for evangelism is the love of Christ, we will not resign our task when rejected by sinners. We go for Him, not them.

Christ Prepared His Disciples

The Lord Jesus prepared His disciples to win the lost by using the right motive. He said, *"He that hath my commandments, and keepeth them, he it is that loveth me"* (John 14:21). Love begets love. Christ loved His disciples and, on the basis of their love for Him, He charged them with the vital responsibility of world evangelism. Our obedience to His command is the real proof of our love for Him. The Bible basis for soul winning is the love of Christ. The Word of God clearly states, *"For this is the love of God, that we keep his commandments"* (I John 5:3). He has commanded us to go.

THE CONDITION OF THE UNSAVED

A doctor by the name of Jonas Salk devoted much of his life to the discovery of a vaccine to cure polio. His life's efforts were rewarded by the discovery of the vaccine. Imagine for a moment that after Dr. Salk discovered the vaccine, he withheld it from all those who needed it. Unthinkable? Yes, but there are multitudes of Christians with lost and dying humanity at their doorsteps, and they never make any effort to tell them of the Savior. To have means to owe. Those who know the Lord Jesus owe those who do not know.

The introduction to the gospel is the fact that God is a holy God. There can be no Good News without the bad news that men are lost in their sin and separated from a holy God.

SYMPTOMS OF SIN-SICKNESS

The tragic symptoms of sin-sickness call us to soul winning. The symptoms of the sin-sick are many. A few that most of us recognize are:

Emptiness

Men without Christ are empty. There is no way that a life without Christ can be complete. The Bible says, *"But as many as received him, to them gave he power to become the sons of God, even to them that believe on his name"* (John 1:12). It is when men receive Christ that the emptiness of life is filled.

Without Meaning

Multitudes could be called "aimless wanderers." The lost man has no real purpose or direction. He may find temporary meaning in a material goal, but the deepest longings of his heart will not find satisfaction without Christ. The Lord Jesus said, *"I am the way."* His way is the only way to find meaning in this life.

Fear of Death

To the unsaved, death is a frightening journey into the unknown. To the Christian, it is the door that opens into an eternity with the Lord Jesus. Eternal life begins

> *So often the need of mankind is considered to be the highest motive for personal evangelism; but according to the Word of God, our highest motive is the love of Christ.*

when we trust the Lord Jesus Christ as our personal Savior. It does not begin at death. He has promised to give us grace and strength to overcome this great fear. He said, *"I am the resurrection, and the life: he that believeth in me, though he were dead, yet shall he live: and whosoever liveth and believeth in me shall never die"* (John 11:25-26).

Lack of Inner Peace

I once heard someone say that he felt as if he were living in a pressure cooker. The lost man has no peace in his soul. The Lord Jesus is the only One who can bring this peace. He said to His disciples after He had announced to them that He would be crucified, *"Peace I leave with you, my peace I give unto you: not as the world giveth, give I unto you. Let not your heart be troubled, neither let it be afraid"* (John 14:27).

Loneliness

There is no friend like the Lord Jesus. The unsaved man does not have a constant companion who will never leave or forsake him. Christians have such a friend.

The sin disease reflects itself through many symptoms in our society. Christ takes care of more than the symptoms. He is the answer for the disease.

THE BIBLE DECLARES

The Bible is very plain in declaring the condition of those without Christ.

Lost

> *"For the Son of man is come to seek and to save that which was lost."*
>
> Luke 19:10

Perishing

> *"For God so loved the world, that he gave his only begotten Son, that whosoever believeth in him should not perish, but have everlasting life."*
>
> John 3:16

Under God's Wrath

> *"He that believeth on the Son hath everlasting life: and he that believeth not the Son shall not see life; but the wrath of God abideth on him."*
>
> John 3:36

Condemned Already

"He that believeth on him is not condemned: but he that believeth not is condemned already, because he hath not believed in the name of the only begotten Son of God."

John 3:18

Without Hope

"That at that time ye were without Christ, being aliens from the commonwealth of Israel, and strangers from the covenants of promise, having no hope, and without God in the world."

Ephesians 2:12

Blinded by the Devil

"But if our gospel be hid, it is hid to them that are lost: in whom the god of this world hath blinded the minds of them which believe not, lest the light of the glorious gospel of Christ, who is the image of God, should shine unto them."

II Corinthians 4:3-4

Our highest motive in the matter of soul winning must be one of love for our Savior, and out of this love comes a desire to obey His command.

On the Road to Hell

"Enter ye in at the strait gate: for wide is the gate, and broad is the way, that leadeth to destruction, and many there be which go in thereat."

Matthew 7:13

Dead Already in Sin

"And you hath he quickened, who were dead in trespasses and sins."

Ephesians 2:1

SILENCE IS SIN

If we know the Lord Jesus as our personal Savior, we are indebted to tell the unsaved of Him. The apostle Paul wrote to Rome,

I am debtor both to the Greeks, and to the Barbarians; both to the wise, and to the unwise. So, as much as in me is, I am ready to preach the gospel to you that are at Rome also. For I am not ashamed of the gospel of Christ: for it is the power of God unto salvation to every one that believeth; to the Jew first, and also to the Greek (Romans 1:14-16).

The world owes us nothing, but we owe the world the message of salvation. There is a powerful story in the Bible in the book of II Kings chapter seven that illustrates the sin of silence. Beginning with verse three, the story tells of four lepers who sat at the entrance of the city gate. Their city, the city of Samaria, was under the siege of the Syrian army. People inside the city were dying of hunger. These lepers decided to leave their place at the gate of the city and enter the camp of the enemy. To their glad surprise, the Syrian army had been frightened away by the Lord and the lepers found everything they needed. Suddenly, they remembered the starving masses back in the city and they said one to another, *"We do not well: this day is a day of good tidings, and we hold our peace"* (II Kings 7:9). They returned to the city and told the good news. Likewise, our day is a day of much tragedy, but we have found the Good News. It is a terrible sin to be silent when we have the Good News that the world needs to hear. It is as wrong not to do right as it is to do wrong.

It is just as ugly and sinful to do nothing when it is in our power to do good, as it is to go out and deliberately do wrong. The Bible says, *"Therefore to him that knoweth to do good, and doeth it not, to him it is sin"* (James 4:17).

AWAY WITH EXCUSES

The only way to start soul winning is to start! Every Christian has a story to tell. It is the story of how he came to know the Lord Jesus Christ as his Savior. Many excuses have been the offered for not attempting to win the lost. These excuses will not stand up when we stand before God. Most every excuse offered will fall into one of the following categories:

IS IT REALLY MY RESPONSIBILITY?

It has already been clearly stated from the Bible that soul winning is every Christian's responsibility. The Lord has placed this matter of highest importance in our hands. He has chosen men to tell the gospel story. Only the ransomed can tell the story of the soul set free. As Christians, if we do not tell others how to be saved, the simple yet profound truth is—they will not hear! It is our responsibility.

MEN WILL NOT LISTEN

While it is true that there is a great deal of indifference on the part of some people, many will listen. Many are waiting to hear the Good News. The Lord is doing a work in their hearts. The first time anyone clearly gave the gospel to me, I trusted the Lord Jesus Christ as my personal Savior. The Lord had prepared my heart to hear His Word.

Some speak of their fear of offending those who do not want to hear when the real problem is not our fear of offending others, it is our fear of others offending us. Remember, we have a story to tell even if they will not listen. Be willing to be so identified with Christ that you bear His reproach.

We have been given divine authority to tell others of the Savior. We have a right, a God-given right, to go into all the world and preach the gospel to every creature. We need not wait for an invitation. We have already been commanded to go. Our Lord knows the need of mankind, and He has called us to speak to that need. Men realize that there is something missing in their lives, even though they do not recognize what that missing element happens to be. It is our responsibility as Christians to tell them that it is Christ they need.

I AM NOT ABLE

Perhaps in no other area do so many feel such a weakness as in this area, yet our God has commanded us to go. He loves us so much that He would not charge us with a responsibility without providing for us the necessary power for the task. Our strength comes from the indwelling Holy Spirit. He gives us power. He makes us able. He speaks through us as we yield to Him. He gives us the wisdom we so desperately need. Our fear of failure can be used to thrust us to total dependence on the Holy Spirit for soul-winning enablement. He has said, *"Follow me, and I will make you fishers of men"* (Matthew 4:19).

Our purpose is to win souls. Our program is to seek out the lost. Our position is that of an ambassador for Christ. Our proclamation is the gospel. Our power is the Holy Spirit.

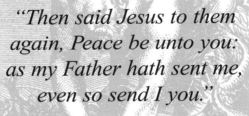

"Then said Jesus to them again, Peace be unto you: as my Father hath sent me, even so send I you."

John 20:21

THE GREAT COMMISSION

t is an amazing truth that the one thing God has given us to do is our single greatest failure. In Matthew chapter twenty-eight, we have one of the most familiar portions of Scripture in all the Word of God. The subject is the Great Commission. In most churches today, we work at just about everything but pursuing souls. If we do talk about pursuing souls, that is usually as far as it gets.

In our towns and great cities, there are more people lost without Christ than at any other time in our history. Also, there is less evangelistic activity and personal soul winning than at any other time. What is happening? One might find a singing event, pageant, or some so-called Christian function to attend, but how much of what is going on in God's name has God truly given us to do?

The Lord Jesus, with nail-pierced hands, gave the Great Commission. May God stir our hearts to a new beginning of obedience to Him in this matter.

The Bible says in Matthew 28:16-20,

> *Then the eleven disciples went away into Galilee, into a mountain where Jesus had appointed them. And when they saw him, they worshipped him: but some doubted. And Jesus came and spake unto them, saying, All power is given unto me in heaven and in earth. Go ye therefore, and teach all nations, baptizing them in the name of the Father, and of the Son and of the Holy Ghost: teaching them to observe all things whatsoever I have commanded you: and, lo, I am with you alway, even unto the end of the world. Amen.*

Jesus Christ spoke to His disciples, and He gave them what we now call the Great Commission. This particular account in Matthew twenty-eight is perhaps the most familiar of the records that God gave concerning the Great Commission. The Great Commission is found one time in each of the Gospels–Matthew, Mark, Luke, and John–and once in the book of Acts. One can take any of these records of the Great Commission and each of them will stand by itself as a call from God to go into all the world and preach the gospel to every creature.

It should not be the burden of a church to build buildings, have a Christian school, or hold special meetings. The burden of the church must be to fulfill the Great Commission by bringing people to Jesus Christ and seeing them obey Christ in baptism and continue to follow the Lord Jesus. The physical things we see that surround us in the church are the by-products of the great work of soul winning. These things should never be the goal, only the by-products.

Unfortunately, in so many churches, we become caretakers of the by-products. Churches are not busy with the work of the gospel.

FIVE PARTS MAKE THE WHOLE

As we take each of the five times the Great Commission is recorded, finding the particular thing that can be found in each of them, and put the five parts together to make the whole, we come to understand what is truly involved in this Great Commission. Let us attempt to take these five things in the order in which Christ gave them. It will not be the order we find in our Bibles–Matthew, Mark, Luke, John, and Acts; but in the order in which they occurred.

The Lord Jesus Christ came to earth, was born of a virgin, lived a sinless life, went to Calvary, bled and died, came forth bodily from the grave alive forevermore, and ascended to heaven. Jesus Christ ever liveth at the right hand of the Father interceding for us. He rose from the dead and spent forty days with His disciples before ascending to heaven. There were forty days from His resurrection to His ascension. During those forty days He gave this Great Commission. Two references were given on the day of His resurrection. Two references were given on the day of His ascension. The center reference, or third reference, was given in Galilee some time during those forty days.

> *The burden of the church must be to fulfill the Great Commission by bringing people to Jesus Christ and seeing them obey Christ in baptism and continue to follow the Lord Jesus.*

WE ARE SENT BY DIVINE AUTHORITY

The first reference we find in the chronology of events is in the Gospel according to John. In John chapter twenty, ten frightened disciples were gathered in an upper room. Thomas was not with them, and Judas, of course, was not with them. Christ was resurrected from the dead. The Bible says in John 20:19-21,

> *Then the same day at evening, being the first day of the week, when the doors were shut where the disciples were assembled for the fear of the Jews, came Jesus and stood in the midst, and saith unto them, Peace be unto you. And when he had so said, he shewed unto them his hands and his side. Then were the disciples glad, when they saw the Lord. Then said Jesus to them again, Peace be unto you: as my Father hath sent me, even so send I you.*

This seems to be the very first time after His death, burial, and resurrection that Christ gave this Great Commission. The disciples were in a room gathered together when Christ appeared in the midst of them and said, *"As my Father hath sent me, even so send I you."* He established this great truth, *"As my Father hath sent me, even so send I you."* In other words, this Great Commission does not begin with the need of man. It does not begin with some sad story about a lost child. This Great Commission begins in the heart of God. The foundation for this Commission is in the heart of God. The Lord Jesus said, *"As my Father hath sent me, even so send I you."*

Almost every missionary report begins with the story of witnessing to some neglected group of human beings. This is not really where God starts the Great Commission. He starts it from His own heart. It all begins with God. This is the essential point. Not one of us has the compassion, concern, and care to continually go after people simply for their sake. After a while, we become annoyed with people and even disgusted with certain individuals. However, our motive is not them, but Him. The Lord Jesus said, *"As my Father hath sent me, even so send I you."* God said, "Go for Me." It starts with the heart of God. When we do what we should do in the Great Commission, we are obeying God. When we do not do what we should do, we are disobeying God. We have been given authority to go. This authority is from our God.

YE ARE WITNESSES

The second time this Commission is given is in the Gospel according to Luke. Here we find an amazing statement. On the same day of His resurrection, later in the day, Christ appeared again to His disciples. This time two from the Emmaus road were with the others. As they gathered together, it must have been very late because in reading Luke chapter twenty-four, Christ had traveled with these disciples on the Emmaus road. As He traveled with them, He made Himself known to them. As He made Himself known, they became very excited. Even though it was late in the day, they went all the way back from Emmaus to Jerusalem and announced to the disciples that Christ had risen and that they had seen and walked with Him on the road to Emmaus. Christ appeared to His disciples again this second time on the day of His resurrection. The Word of God says in Luke 24:36, *"And as they thus spake, Jesus himself stood in the midst of them, and saith unto them, Peace be unto you."*

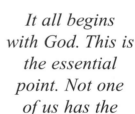

It all begins with God. This is the essential point. Not one of us has the compassion, concern, and care to continually go after people simply for their sake.

Then Christ said to them in verses forty-six through forty-eight,

> *Thus it is written, and thus it behoved Christ to suffer, and to rise from the dead the third day: and that repentance and remission of sins should be preached in his name among all nations, beginning in Jerusalem. And ye are witnesses of these things.*

He specifically said, *"Ye are witnesses of these things."* The Lord said, *"Thus it is written, and thus it behoved Christ to suffer, and to rise from the dead the third day."* He then said to His disciples, *"And ye are witnesses of these things."* Often in an attempt to explain the statement, *"Ye are witnesses of these things,"* people speak of the need to witness. This is exactly opposite of what Christ meant. The Lord Jesus told them that it was written that He should suffer. He would go to Calvary to bleed and die and rise from the dead the third day. He declared to them, *"Ye are witnesses of these things."* Before we can witness, we must be witnesses. There are many who are trying to witness who are not witnesses. The Lord Jesus said, *"Ye are witnesses of these things."* The *noun* comes before the *verb*. We must be witnesses in order to witness. You are never going to be able to witness to anyone until you know that Christ is real in your life.

> *The Lord Jesus said,* "Ye are witnesses of these things." *The* noun comes *before the* verb. *We must be witnesses in order to witness.*

As a young student at the University of Tennessee in Knoxville, the Lord was real to me. I had to complete a certain course of study in order to get the degree I was seeking. I took courses in anthropology, biology, and geology. I sat in those classrooms and listened to professors who attempted to be so convincing. Oil companies spent millions of dollars for programs and films that portrayed evolution in such a dramatic way. I saw hundreds of classmates being brainwashed, but nothing that those professors said, no film they showed, no slide presentation they gave could take away from me what Christ had done and who He was in my life. I was a personal witness of what Christ had done in my life.

The work of God will be done through those who are *"witnesses of these things."* The word *witness* is an amazing word. It comes from the same root word from which we get the English word *martyr*. It means "to die." Before we are the witnesses we should be, we must die to self.

THE LORD JESUS IS WITH US AS WE WITNESS

The third time this Great Commission is given is in Matthew chapter twenty-eight. The Bible says in Matthew 28:16-20,

> *Then the eleven disciples went away in to Galilee, into a mountain where Jesus had appointed them. And when they saw him, they worshipped him: but some doubted. And Jesus came and spake unto them, saying, All power is given unto me in heaven and in earth. Go ye therefore, and teach all nations, baptizing them in the name of the Father, and of the Son, and of the Holy Ghost: teaching them to observe all things whatsoever I have commanded you: and, lo, I am with you alway, even unto the end of the world. Amen.*

Note the word *"go"* in verse nineteen and the little word *"lo"* in the center of verse twenty. I have circled these two words in my Bible. I have drawn a line connecting the two words, *"go"* and *"lo."* When the Lord Jesus gave this part of the Commission after His resurrection, some time during those forty days before His ascension, He revealed something He did not reveal at other times. By comparing Scripture with Scripture and reading I Corinthians chapter fifteen, the reference in Matthew chapter twenty-eight appears to be the time when there were five hundred followers assembled listening to Christ at one time. When Paul wrote the first Corinthian letter about twenty-seven years after the resurrection of Christ, he said there were more than half of the five hundred still alive who were witnesses of the Lord Jesus after His resurrection.

The Lord Jesus let His followers know that His work was not accomplished by the power of oratory, training, or seminars, but by His presence and power.

The Lord Jesus commanded them to go into all the world, preach the gospel, and teach all nations. When He said, *"Go,"* He then said, *"And lo, I am with you alway."* In other words He said, "You do not have to do this alone; I will go with you." The Holy Spirit is not confined to a location as Christ was in His robe of flesh. As the disciples went in every direction, the Lord, in the Person of the Holy Spirit, went with them.

Our God has sent us. We are His witnesses. Christ said, *"Go"* and *"lo, I am with you."* The Lord Jesus let His followers know that His work was not accomplished by the power of oratory, training, or seminars, but by His presence and power. The continuing work of Christ in the Person of the Holy Spirit was a work that allowed the Lord Jesus to go with His disciples no matter where they went with the gospel message.

MIRACLES TAKE PLACE AS THE GOSPEL IS PROCLAIMED

The fourth reference to this Great Commission is in the book of Mark. The Bible says in Mark 16:15-18,

> *And he said unto them, Go ye into all the world, and preach the gospel to every creature. He that believeth and is baptized shall be saved; but he that believeth not shall be damned. And these signs shall follow them that believe; in my name shall they cast out devils; they shall speak with new tongues; they shall take up serpents; and if they drink any deadly thing, it shall not hurt them; they shall lay hands on the sick, and they shall recover.*

Note the expression found in verse seventeen, *"And these signs shall follow them that believe."* This fourth time the Great Commission was given, it was given on the day of Christ's ascension. The first two references were given on the day of His resurrection; the account in Matthew was given sometime during the forty days Christ was with His disciples; and this one in Mark was given on the day of His ascension. Remember, as recorded in John, that the Lord Jesus said, *"As my Father hath sent me."* This Great Commission begins with God and not with man. The idea of marketing the church begins with man and not with

This Great Commission begins with God and not with man.

God. We do not have to go out and find what people need. God knows what people need, and He put what they need in His Book. Give people the Bible. The Lord Jesus said in John 2:25 that He knew what was in man.

In Luke, Christ reveals to us that we are witnesses. In Matthew, we see that, as we *"go," "lo"* He is with us. His presence is promised for His work. In the Gospel according to Mark, He reveals what is going to happen as the gospel is preached. Marvelous miracles are going to take place. This is not about sign gifts but about changed lives. Men who have been bound by alcohol all their lives are set free the moment they get saved. Story after story could be told about people who were addicted to drugs, alcohol, and other unimaginable things, but they came to the Lord Jesus, and He changed their lives. We have a God who can change people's lives.

THERE IS NO PLACE TO STOP

The fifth reference is in the book of Acts. Of course, this took place on the day of Christ's ascension. God's Word says in Acts 1:6-8,

> *When they therefore were come together, they asked of him, saying, Lord, wilt thou at this time restore again the kingdom to Israel? And he said unto them, It is not for you to know the times or the seasons, which the Father hath put in his own power. But ye shall receive power, after that the Holy Ghost is come upon you: and ye shall be witnesses unto me both in Jersualem, and in all Judæa, and in Samaria, and unto the uttermost part of the earth.*

Parts of the Great Commission were given on five different occasions, in five different meetings. The first two times it was given on the day of Christ's resurrection, the last two times on the day of His ascension, and once sometime during the forty days He was with His disciples after His resurrection. Each time something different was revealed to complete the whole.

In verse eight of Acts chapter one the Bible says, *"And unto the uttermost part of the earth."* There is no stopping place. We are to press on to the ends of the earth and the islands of the sea, to the uttermost part of the earth. There is no place to stop. There is no time to stop.

Let us give, go, pray, work and do all we can do that Christ might receive the reward of His suffering. No wonder we call this the Great Commission. In John Christ said, *"As my Father hath sent me."* In Luke He said, *"And ye are witnesses."* In Matthew He commanded us to *"go"* and promised us, *"Lo I am with you alway."* In Mark, people were saved, miracles were seen as lives were changed. In Acts we understand that there is no place to stop until the trumpet sounds for His return. The Lord Jesus said, *"To the uttermost part of the earth."* May God help us to spread the gospel to the uttermost part of the earth. This is His passion.

"Go ye therefore, and teach all nations, baptizing them in the name of the Father, and of the Son, and of the Holy Ghost: teaching them to observe all things whatsoever I have commanded you: and, lo, I am with you alway, even unto the end of the world. Amen."

Matthew 28:19-20

GOD'S BLUEPRINT FOR DEALING WITH ALL MEN

 Before our Lord ascended back to heaven, He left His disciples with His plan for world evangelism. He said,

Go ye therefore, and teach all nations, baptizing them in the name of the Father, and of the Son, and of the Holy Ghost: teaching them to observe all things whatsoever I have commanded you: and, lo, I am with you alway, even unto the end of the world. Amen (Matthew 28:19-20).

As we have seen already, this is a portion of what is often called the Great Commission. It is recorded in each of the Gospel records and in the book of Acts. Actually, we put all accounts together to get the full impact of what Christ commanded us to do. We must look again at how this Great Commission is to be carried out. It must be done with promptness, persistence, and power.

Almost two thousand years have passed since our Lord left the church with the responsibility of giving the gospel to the world. Not only in distant lands do men still live and die without hearing a clear presentation of the gospel, but also in the neighborhoods of churches in our own land, men are living without God and without the gospel message.

WE NEED NO NEW COMMAND

The church needs no new command from Christ. This is not a day for doing new things. It must be a day of obeying the command already given to go into all the world and preach the gospel to every creature. With nail-pierced hands, Christ still points to millions who have never heard. The Bible-believing church must obey the Bible mandate that He has given. The church that is still trying to decide what area to place its emphasis is simply not obeying the command Christ has given. The Lord Jesus Christ said we are to go after souls.

The Lord has a blueprint for us to follow in the work He has given us to do. The early disciples obeyed His command and within one generation, without our modern facilities of travel and without our modern means of the publication of God's Word, the gospel message went from lip to ear until it actually touched all of the Roman Empire.

Step One: Go

Of course, we should set aside time to go after souls, but let us determine to be faithful witnesses–telling the lost of the Savior as we go. The faithful witness is conscious of lost souls. He is seeking the lost and using every means available to bring people to Christ.

Christ said, *"Go ye therefore."* We are to go where people are, from house to store to street, telling people how to be saved. This word *"go"* is the one little word that makes the great difference in soul winning.

Many sincere Christians have questions concerning soul winning. No one can give an answer to these questions that could be considered full or final except the Lord Jesus, but there are some things of great importance that must be mentioned.

We must have assurance of our own salvation and a working knowledge of the Word of God, but there is one thing that is so very simple, yet so absolutely necessary. We must *go* after souls. Many Christians have assurance of their salvation, have memorized what they call the plan of salvation, realize the lost are going to hell, and have even attended good training sessions on how to win the lost, but they never go after souls. We must determine to go.

If we are not going, we are disobeying God. He has commanded us to go. We will gain spiritual understanding of how God can use us in His work as we go. We will see the hopelessness of humanity without Christ. Our hearts will be burdened only as we go. Compassion does not come from the study of facts on soul winning, nor from training sessions on soul winning. It comes from God's heart to our heart as we go soul winning.

> *The church needs no new command from Christ. This is not a day for doing new things. It must be a day of obeying the command already given to go into all the world and preach the gospel to every creature.*

Many Christians have all the Bible truths clearly fixed in their minds, but they possess cold hearts because they do not go. If we desire a burden for souls, then we must go after souls. There is no such thing as great soul winners. There are only those who seek the lost for the Lord Jesus Christ and those who do not.

When God made each believer a messenger of the gospel, He had at heart not only the salvation of the lost, but also what is best for believers. For a Christian to neglect soul winning and not go after souls means that he will become cold, hard, and joyless. Stagnation breeds decay. The Word of God says, *"He that goeth forth and weepeth, bearing precious seed, shall doubtless come again with rejoicing, bringing his sheaves with him"* (Psalm 126:6).

Step Two: Explain the Way of Salvation

The Lord Jesus said, *"Teach all nations."* We are to give a clear presentation of the gospel. Many people have no effectiveness because they do not clearly speak the gospel message. Use terms and language

that people understand. This is absolutely not an appeal to use vulgar street talk and slang language that some so-called "evangelists" are using, but rather a simple plea for the use of terms that are found in God's Word. The Bible speaks of sin, death, hell, eternal life, and of becoming new creatures in Christ Jesus.

> *The personal soul winner must not attempt to be a theologian, but rather a witness of the saving power of the Lord Jesus Christ.*

The personal soul winner must not attempt to be a theologian, but rather a witness of the saving power of the Lord Jesus Christ. A soul winner must use the clear language of the Bible in speaking to people about Christ. Remember, our message is more than proclaiming the facts about the Lord Jesus. It must include a call to personal commitment and surrender to the Lord Jesus Christ. When our Lord said, *"Ye are witnesses of these things,"* He was declaring to His followers that they knew firsthand what Christ could do for others because of what He had done in their lives.

Step Three: Baptize Them

The Bible teaches that the first step of obedience for the new Christian is the step of baptism. The Lord Jesus Christ said,

"Baptizing them in the name of the Father, and of the Son, and of the Holy Ghost." This has no saving power, but this command given to the church to baptize converts identifies the new believer with the Lord Jesus Christ and the local church.

Step Four: Teach Them

We are to reach people with the gospel message and then teach them God's Word. This is the task of the local church. Every new Christian should become faithfully involved in a local, Bible-believing, Bible-preaching church. The Lord said, *"Teaching them to observe all things whatsoever I have commanded you."* Our job is not finished until the evangelized become evangelists! The emphasis of the Bible is on teaching the believer the responsibility he has to follow the Lord Jesus Christ.

OUR GREAT FAILURES

The command given in Matthew 28:19-20 not only shows us the step-by-step plan that we are to follow, but it also points us to our greatest failures in soul-winning work.

Our First Failure

Our number one failure is our failure to go. Good intentions get no one to Christ. We must go! No one will be saved unless we first go. Promise God you will go and speak to the lost of the Savior. Seek the lost.

The reason we do not go is because we are not following Christ. His passion for the lost will become our passion as we follow Him. We are to be conscious of the lost.

Our Second Failure

Our second greatest failure in the work of winning the lost is our failure to give a clear presentation of the gospel message when we do go. It is so easy to be sidetracked. Men must be confronted with the message of Christ and be brought to the place of putting their personal faith in Him for salvation. Men must hear the truth of God's Word concerning their lost condition.

Tell people of the Savior. Do not consider that you are to speak to people about some plan. Tell them of the Person of Christ. As they hear you speak of the Lord Jesus and they desire to know Him, He will make Himself known to them.

Our Third Failure

Many people speak to lost ones about Christ and see those lost ones trust Him for salvation, but they never lead that new convert to follow Christ in believer's baptism. This is our third great failure. It is not right to bring someone to Christ and then never show that person that he should be baptized, publicly declaring his faith in Christ and identifying with the Lord Jesus and the local church.

Our Fourth Failure

The Lord Jesus has taught us that after salvation new Christians should be taught the things He has commanded us to do. It is our responsibility to work with these babes in Christ, teaching them the things of God and encouraging them to faithfully attend the church. We fail so often to follow the command of Christ in this area. As the new Christian follows Christ, he will be faithful to the things his Lord loves.

DEALING WITH ALL PEOPLE

Every individual is in one of these four groups. Every time we knock on a door or speak to someone about Christ, we will find him in one of these groups.

The Person No One Has Ever Gone After

We must purpose in our hearts to go after him and tell him of Christ.

The One Who Has Been Gone After but Never Saved

We must give this individual a clear presentation of the gospel and invite him to trust Christ as his personal Savior.

The Christian Who Has Never Been Baptized

There are many people who have received Christ as their personal Savior but have never followed Him in believer's baptism since they have been saved. We must show them from God's Word that the first step of obedience for the new Christian is the step of identifying himself with Christ and His church by following Him in baptism.

The Saved Person Who Is Not Faithfully Attending a Local, Bible-Believing Church

So many say they have received Christ as personal Savior and have been baptized, yet they do not attend a local, Bible-believing church faithfully. The Lord Jesus said, *"Teaching them to observe all things whatsoever I have commanded you."* This is where the local church comes in. This involves faithfully attending a local Bible-believing church and growing in the grace and knowledge of the Lord Jesus Christ.

Everyone with whom we come into contact will fall into one of these four categories. First, there is the one who has never been gone after for Christ. Second, there is the person who has been gone after but is still unsaved. Third, there is the individual who has been gone after and saved but has never followed the Lord Jesus Christ in believer's baptism since he has been saved. Fourth, there is the person who has been gone after, saved, and baptized, but is not faithfully attending a local, Bible-believing, Bible-preaching church.

In Matthew 28:19-20, the Lord Jesus gives us His plan or blueprint for dealing with all people. To carry out this plan, He promises His power and His presence. In this entire matter, let us seek the Lord Jesus for the discernment we need to instruct people in the ways of the Lord.

"Jesus answered and said unto her, Whosoever drinketh of this water shall thirst again: but whosoever drinketh of the water that I shall give him shall never thirst; but the water that I shall give him shall be in him a well of water springing up into everlasting life."

John 4:13-14

CHRIST, OUR EXAMPLE

 he Lord Jesus Christ is our supreme example in soul winning. His consuming passion was *"to seek and to save that which was lost."* The motive behind His dealing with all people was to win them to Himself. If we desire to be effective in the work of winning the lost to Him, we must study His life and dealings with the unsaved. It is impossible to adequately describe the Lord Jesus as a soul winner, but it is necessary for us to attempt to find the things demonstrated in His life and ministry that we need in order to do this most important work He has called us to do—the winning of souls.

With this in mind, let us take one of the most familiar Bible stories in the life of the Master Soul Winner and find in it what is helpful to us in winning the lost. The example we have chosen is found in the fourth chapter of the Gospel according to John, as the Lord Jesus dealt with the woman at the well. Read thoroughly this biblical account.

HE WENT OUT OF HIS WAY TO WITNESS TO THE WOMAN

He did not take the normal route on this journey. He went out of His way to speak to this lost sinner. The Bible states in John 4:4, *"He must needs go through Samaria."* There is a divine compulsion here. We feel His concern for this lost woman. Most of us are willing to witness if lost people happen to cross our path, but the Lord Jesus taught us by His example that we should go out of our way to find the unsaved. We are not only to take opportunities, we are to place ourselves in His hands and know that He brings us in contact with those who need Him and leads us to the lost. Let us seek them as one would seek to find something that is lost.

HE SPOKE WITH HER ABOUT HER SOUL EVEN WHEN HE DID NOT FEEL LIKE IT

The Bible says in John 4:6, *"Jesus therefore, being wearied."* He was *"wearied."* Most of us do only what we feel like doing. We pray, read our Bibles, and witness when we feel like it. The Lord Jesus rose above His weariness and spoke to this woman. We must learn to follow His example and rise above our feelings and do what is right whether we feel like it or not. We must live by principles and not by feelings.

HE WAS CONCERNED ABOUT ALL PEOPLE

The woman in this chapter was not exactly the type that most churches are looking for, but Christ sought her. If we desire Christ-likeness in soul winning, we must stop considering who would fit in our churches and start asking, "To whom are we responsible?" We are to love all people.

HE BEGAN THE CONVERSATION CASUALLY

The Bible says in John 4:7, *"There cometh a woman of Samaria to draw water: Jesus saith unto her, Give me to drink."* The Lord Jesus met this woman in the heat of the day and began speaking with her about a very normal topic of conversation. We must work with people at their level, conversing with them in a way that opens the door to witnessing.

HE TURNED THE CONVERSATION TO SPIRITUAL THINGS

Notice what the Lord Jesus Christ said in verse ten, *"If thou knewest the gift of God, and who it is that saith to thee, Give me to drink; thou wouldest have asked of him, and he would have given thee living water."* In order for people to come to Christ, they must be confronted with spiritual matters. This starts as the conversation turns to spiritual things. Our Lord did just that when He dealt with the woman at the well.

HE TOLD HER OF HIS POWER TO GIVE ETERNAL LIFE

In John 4:13-14 God's Word says,

> *Jesus answered and said unto her, Whosoever drinketh of this water shall thirst again: But whosoever drinketh of the water that I shall give him shall never*

*thirst; but the water that I shall give him shall be in him
a well of water springing up into everlasting life.*

To be sick and have no cure is a hopeless state for this life. To be
sin-sick and have no Savior is a hopeless state for eternity. Christ is
our hope. He has the power to give eternal life. The unsaved must be
made aware of this. Our work as Christians is to speak with people
about the Lord Jesus Christ and His power to save.

HE LED HER TO AN AWARENESS OF HER SPIRITUAL NEED

The Bible says in John 4:16-18,

*Jesus saith unto her, Go, call thy husband, and come
hither. The woman answered and said, I have no husband.
Jesus said unto her, Thou hast well said, I have no
husband: for thou hast had five husbands; and he whom
thou now hast is not thy husband: in that saidst thou truly.*

We seek a doctor when we are sick. We will never seek the Savior
until we realize that we are sin-sick. Men must be made aware of
their spiritual need. Without Christ all people are bound for hell,
dead in trespasses and sins.

HE REFUSED TO BE SIDETRACKED FROM HIS PURPOSE

God's Word says in John 4:19-26,

*The woman saith unto him, Sir, I perceive that thou
art a prophet. Our fathers worshipped in this mountain;
and ye say, that in Jerusalem is the place where men
ought to worship. Jesus saith unto her, Woman, believe*

me, the hour cometh, when ye shall neither in this mountain, nor yet at Jerusalem, worship the Father. Ye worship ye know not what: we know what we worship: for salvation is of the Jews. But the hour cometh, and now is, when the true worshippers shall worship the Father in spirit and in truth: for the Father seeketh such to worship him. God is a Spirit: and they that worship him must worship him in spirit and in truth. The woman saith unto him, I know that Messias cometh, which is called Christ: when he is come, he will tell us all things. Jesus saith unto her, I that speak unto thee am he.

One of Satan's tricks is to sidetrack the soul winner. Christ was so consumed by His purpose that He refused to be sidetracked from it.

THE WOMAN TRUSTED HIM AS HER SAVIOR AND BEGAN TO WIN SOULS

We read in John 4:28-29,

The woman then left her waterpot, and went her way into the city, and saith to the men, Come, see a man, which told me all things that ever I did: is not this the Christ?

This is the victory. This is our reason for witnessing—to bring glory to the Lord and to win the lost. Our goal must be to see the lost saved and have them telling others of the Savior. There are a number of things found in the life of the Lord Jesus in the opening verses of chapter four, leading up to His conversation with the woman at the well, that need to be in the lives of all those who desire to win souls.

If we are truly born again, we have within us the secret to soul winning. The Master Soul Winner, the Lord Jesus, lives in us. He will speak through us and make us the soul winners He desires for us to be as we yield our lives to Him.

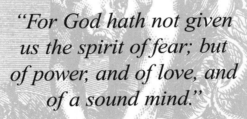

"For God hath not given us the spirit of fear; but of power, and of love, and of a sound mind."

II Timothy 1:7

OVERCOMING FEAR IN SOUL WINNING

 e realize as Christians that we are to witness to others. We are commanded by Christ. In addition to this, we have in our hearts a call from within to witness because of what we have experienced in our own lives. This is heightened as we come in contact each day with individuals who are living meaningless lives and have no hope, yet we are afraid. Many critics of personal soul winning need to stop their criticism and go with boldness in the name of the Lord Jesus, telling the lost of Christ.

AFRAID OF WHAT?

There are a number of fears that trouble people when it comes to the matter of witnessing to the lost.

THE FEAR OF PERSONAL REJECTION

So often people say that they do not witness to others for fear of offending them. The real problem is not that we are afraid of offending people—we are afraid people are going to offend us.

THE FEAR OF DIFFERENT LIFESTYLES

We have developed in our minds the thought that certain individuals will not listen to what we have to say about Christ. Some fear the wealthy. Some fear the educated. Others fear witnessing to those who have the appearance of the "rebel" culture in our society. Remember, it is not our business to try to guess which individuals will hear and will not hear. It is our responsibility to give the clear gospel message to all men. It is not our responsibility to sample the soil but to sow the seed.

It is not our responsibility to sample the soil but to sow the seed.

THE FEAR OF NOT KNOWING HOW

If we are ever going to bring the lost to Christ, we must start at some point. I started by passing out gospel tracts. Later, I stumbled through a brief presentation of my own personal testimony. All the while I was trying to learn a simple way of explaining to an individual that he was lost, that Christ died for his sins, and that he could be saved by putting his faith in the finished work of Christ on the cross. I simply memorized a few Scripture passages that pointed out each thing the sinner must believe. I learned how to locate those Scriptures in a New Testament, to read them to the unsaved, and to make a brief comment of explanation about each one. Anyone can enlarge on a beginning like this. The point is, we must start somewhere.

THE FEAR OF FAILURE

Many Christians have a false idea of the meaning of success in soul winning. If we have gone in the power of the Holy Spirit, given a clear presentation of the gospel, and brought the individual to the place of putting his faith in Christ to save him, then that is all we can do. We have not failed when the person to whom we have witnessed rejects Christ. It would be failure not to have gone after the lost one.

FEAR IS A COMMON THING

The Christian who desires to win souls needs to learn that feelings of fear are very normal. They can be used to a great advantage. The truth is, we can learn that these fears are very normal feelings and that God will enable us to overcome them. Our fears are overcome only as we walk with the Lord and abide in His presence. The Lord promises in His Word that His *"strength is made perfect in weakness"* (II Corinthians 12:9).

Our fears are overcome only as we walk with the Lord and abide in His presence.

THE HOLY SPIRIT WILL BE AT WORK

The Holy Spirit indwells every Christian and empowers him to tell others of the Savior. The Holy Spirit will help us overcome fear. The Bible says, *"For God hath not given us the spirit of fear; but of power, and of love, and of a sound mind"* (II Timothy 1:7).

The Holy Spirit will also work in the heart of the unbeliever to whom we witness, convicting him of sin and his need for the Lord Jesus. Our jod works on both ends. He empowers the witness and convicts the sinner. Remember what Christ said when He commissioned His disciples, *"And, lo, I am with you alway"* (Matthew 28:20).

CRITICAL AREAS IN SOUL WINNING

As we conclude this chapter, there are a number of critical areas that soul winners need to recognize. A long list could possibly be given at this point, but the "hard places" in personal soul winning basically fall into three categories. If we can prayerfully prepare for these three critical areas, we will be able to be more effective in the work of winning the lost.

THE APPROACH

We are ambassadors for Christ. We represent the Lord Jesus Christ to a lost world. We speak for Him. Most people have a difficult time making new acquaintances and starting conversations. We must learn the best ways of opening a conversation with an unsaved person.

Be Yourself

Be Genuine

Move Toward the Person With Purpose and Direction

Maintain Eye Contact

Be Pleasant

Be Enthusiastic

Give Your Name

Be Straight Forward With What You Are Doing

Offer Printed Material

Begin Casual Conversation

During the approach, if someone is rude to the soul winner, we must remember what God's Word says, *"A soft answer turneth away wrath: but grievous words stir up anger"* (Proverbs 15:1). Very politely apologize to the person and with kindness state your purpose again. You may have the opportunity to give your personal testimony at this point.

TURNING THE CONVERSATION TO SPIRITUAL THINGS

Satan is pleased when we talk on and on with unsaved people and never present a clear presentation of the gospel to them. We must discern the true spiritual condition of the individual before we can help him. In order for this to be done, we must turn the conversation to spiritual things. We will be empowered by the Holy Spirit of God as we begin to speak to people about the Lord Jesus Christ. Once the conversation has turned to a spiritual topic, the way of salvation can be given. Most often the direct approach to this matter should be followed. Simply ask, "Have you ever personally invited the Lord Jesus Christ into your heart?" or "Do you know for sure if you died today that you would go to heaven?"

Some topics that help turn the conversation to spiritual things are:

> *Church Attendance*
>
> *World Conditions*
>
> *Family*
>
> *Eternity*
>
> *Bible Study*

Always follow these topics with the direct question about salvation.

Some may have more difficulty in these areas than others. Remember, God wants to use us to get the gospel to the lost. He will enable us to overcome all our fears.

DRAWING THE NET

After the way of salvation has been given, the unsaved person should be brought to the place of trusting Christ as his personal Savior. Let us lovingly press the matter of trusting Christ as Savior and remember that salvation is of the Lord. It is our responsibility to go in the power of the Holy Spirit, give a clear presentation of the gospel, and bring the person to whom we are witnessing to the place of receiving or rejecting Jesus Christ. When we present the gospel, we have a responsibility to ask for a verdict. There is no neutral ground. A man must receive or reject the Lord Jesus Christ.

After the way of salvation has been given, the unsaved person should be brought to the place of trusting Christ as his personal Savior.

The Lord Jesus said in Matthew 4:19, *"Follow me and I will make you fishers of men."* The crisis with the fisherman is the landing of the fish, whether by net or by line. So it is with the fishers of men. The unsaved person must be brought to the place of personally trusting Christ as his Savior. Remember that most people are utterly ignorant of God's salvation. We must put our faith in the finished work of Christ. People do not know how to pray. They do not understand commonly used Christian terminology such as "Turn it over to the Lord," "saved," or "born again." We must be able to explain to them with the enabling of the Holy Spirit how to be saved. Here are some helpful things to remember:

Be sure the person understands the way of salvation.

Explain to the person that we are separated from God because of our sin.

Ask, "Do you believe God will keep His Word and save you if you ask Him?"

Pray together. This does not need to be a long prayer.

Go over God's promise to save.

Instruct the person to pray.

Lead the person in prayer if necessary.

Ask the person if he has prayed for forgiveness of sin and if he is trusting Christ alone for salvation.

Point him to God's Word (Romans 10:13).

Remind the person that we are saved by faith, not feelings.

Show the person God's promise to save.

"And I give unto them eternal life; and they shall never perish, neither shall any man pluck them out of my hand. My Father, which gave them me, is greater than all; and no man is able to pluck them out of my Father's hand."

John 10:28-29

Eternal life begins when we trust the Lord Jesus Christ as our personal Savior.

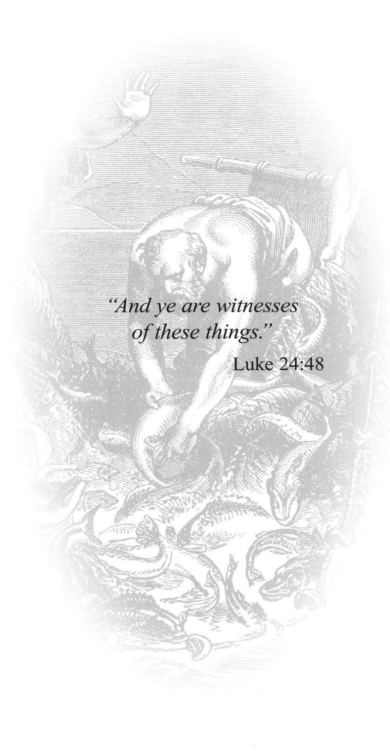

*"And ye are witnesses
of these things."*

Luke 24:48

EVERY CHRISTIAN HAS A STORY TO TELL

 he Lord Jesus said, *"Ye are witnesses of these things."* Every Christian has a story to tell. That story is the Christian's personal testimony. Our personal testimony is one of the most powerful tools that can be used in soul winning. A Christian's testimony involves telling another person what his life was like before he met the Lord Jesus, how he came to know Christ, and what it means now to live the Christian life. Although the details of testimonies vary from person to person, certain common elements exist in every Christian's testimony.

MY LIFE BEFORE RECEIVING CHRIST AS MY PERSONAL SAVIOR

Remember, the lost need Christ because they are sinners by nature. They are separated from God because of their sin, and the direction of all lost men is away from God. God's Word says in Isaiah 53:6, *"All we like sheep have gone astray; we have turned every one to his own way."* When telling your personal testimony, it is not necessary to go into detail concerning sinful things you have done. Some people seem to take great pride in all the terrible things they did before they became Christians. This is not Christ-honoring, and it leaves some people with the idea that only the very bad people need to be saved. The morally upright man who is without Christ thinks he is not bad enough to need to be saved after hearing someone "brag" on his sins when giving a testimony.

HOW I CAME TO KNOW THE LORD JESUS AS MY PERSONAL SAVIOR

We must learn to tell our salvation story in clear, simple terms that are easily understood. Make the salvation experience very plain. Men are saved by asking God to forgive their sin and putting their faith in Christ to save them. The details surrounding the salvation experience will not be the same for every individual. We must be careful not to have people expecting the exact same circumstances that someone else had on the day of his salvation in order to be saved.

Our personal testimony is one of the most powerful tools that can be used in soul winning.

Salvation comes by repentance toward God and faith in the Lord Jesus Christ. Some unusual things may have taken place when you were saved, but you were saved when you put your faith in Christ to save you and not because of surrounding circumstances. When using the term "saved," explain what you mean. Make a point of explaining how you came to know the Lord Jesus Christ as your personal Savior. As the person without Christ listens to your testimony, he should understand how to know the Lord Jesus Christ as his personal Savior.

WHAT CHRIST MEANS TO ME NOW THAT I AM A CHRISTIAN

Most often at this point, we simply state that now we know we are going to heaven when we die. This is wonderful, but we must also tell of the change Christ has made and is making in our life's purpose, our homes, our families, and our friendships. We must tell the unsaved about the peace Christ brings in our hearts each day. Of course, the lost need to know how being a Christian helps us with our life's goals, choosing a life's partner, rearing children, facing failures, and handling great disappointments, but nothing must hide the truth that we are lost, hell-deserving sinners, and the only way of salvation is through the Lord Jesus Christ. Thank God for the absolute assurance that heaven is our eternal home, but we must convey to people how the Christian life helps us here and now while we are on our way to heaven. The Lord Jesus Christ comes to live in the life of every believer.

TELL YOUR STORY IN PUBLIC PLACES

It is important that we become faithful witnesses. Many people may participate in a regular soul-winning activity week after week but never become faithful witnesses. To be a faithful witness means using every available opportunity to speak to people about Christ, specifically speaking to them about how they can know Him as their personal Savior.

We may say that there are two categories of soul winning. One is what we call "planned personal evangelism." This is where specific visits are assigned to people. The entire visitation is planned. The second type of personal evangelism is what we call "contact personal evangelism." This is where Christians speak to the unsaved about Christ wherever or whenever they might contact them in their day-to-day activities. Remember that the Holy Spirit is at work drawing the lost to Christ. As the Lord orders our steps, He brings us in contact with those to whom we are to witness. Our Lord is preparing the hearts of people to receive the gospel.

> *To be a faithful witness means using every available opportunity to speak to people about Christ, specifically speaking to them about how they can know Him as their personal Savior.*

Most churches and most Christians never engage in any type of soul winning except the planned type; but if we can learn how to deal with people about salvation wherever we might contact them, we will begin to see many come to know Christ as Savior. Each day, be a faithful witness of God's saving power. This is where soul winning in public places comes in. This simply means that we seek to win souls wherever we may go.

Have you ever been in a public place and felt as if you should witness, you knew it was your responsibility to witness, but you just did not do it? How can we witness and win the lost in public places?

Many times during my travels, I have had the opportunity to lead people to Christ. Circumstances may seem quite annoying at first. For example, a young pilot was traveling to his flight assignment and sat in the only available seat on the plane which was next to me. The Lord had prepared his heart, and during the flight he trusted Christ as his Savior. I had wanted to quietly rest, but God placed him next to me.

On another occasion, I remember having to take a detour while traveling through Georgia. I stopped at a small grocery to ask for directions, and I had the opportunity to lead a young man to Christ at the grocery store.

I have missed many opportunities by not being a faithful witness, but all of us know that opportunities abound.

BE FRIENDLY AND PERSONABLE IN YOUR FIRST CONTACT

We only have one opportunity to represent Christ well in first impressions. When you go into a place of business, people will look at you and determine certain things about you. We should consciously work at being very personable and kind in our first contact with people in public places. As Christians, we should always represent Christ well. We are witnesses of His grace.

We should consciously work at being very personable and kind in our first contact with people in public places. As Christians, we should always represent Christ well.

LEARN TO TURN THE CONVERSATION TO SPIRITUAL THINGS

Many people talk about the weather, their children, or if business is good or bad, but most of us try to avoid the "risk" subjects of conversation. A "risk" subject of conversation is one that gets you into the sensitive parts of another's life. Subjects such as the weather, sports, and children, to mention only a few, are pretty much "non-risk" subjects. A person's relationship with the Lord is definitely a "risk" subject. However, we must speak to him concerning this matter in order to see him saved. In my opinion, the best way to do this is to be very direct and state, "Let me ask you this question." Then ask the question, "Have you ever personally prayed and invited the Lord Jesus Christ into your life?" There will be someone in that place of business, on the street, at the bus stop, or in the restaurant that you will never see again. Let this thought grip your heart. Be led of the Spirit of God.

NEVER CAUSE A BAD SCENE BY TALKING TOO LOUDLY

The soul winner should not walk into a place and draw all the attention to himself. The Lord Jesus said, *"I will make you fishers of men."* Fishermen do not catch fish by walking up to the water and chasing all the fish away. The same principle works in personal soul winning. Remember, we are talking now about witnessing to individuals in public places. When speaking to individuals, talk in a very soft tone of voice so that one particular person hears you.

TAKE THE CONVERSATION AS FAR AS THE HOLY SPIRIT LEADS

Go as far as the Spirit of God leads. The Holy Spirit, not the eloquent speech of the witness, brings about conviction. Trust God to do a work in hearts.

QUOTE THE SCRIPTURE

When witnessing in public places, it is better, if possible, to quote the Scriptures and not to take your Bible out. We are certainly not ashamed of God's Word. You may wish to use your New Testament. Remember the power of God's Word. When you quote the Scriptures, the people around you may think it is just an ordinary conversation, but actually you are giving out the Word of God. Memorize the Scriptures and the way of salvation.

MAKE EVERY MOMENT COUNT

Remember, you only have a limited amount of time to witness at a bus stop, in an elevator, or in a place of business. You may be able to get some information about people and visit later in their home, or perhaps you can speak thoroughly of the way of salvation and see them saved in the public place. Follow the Lord's leading. You never know what people are going through. The Holy Spirit is at work dealing with the lost person. A person may have been to the doctor that morning and found out that he has a serious illness and may be broken-hearted. The Lord may have sent you by just for that one person. You never know. Our Lord has given us authority to speak to every person and a responsibility to witness everywhere. Work at being more effective in public places. Make every moment count.

BE SURE THE PEOPLE ARE CONVICTED OF SIN AND SHOW A DESIRE TO KNOW CHRIST

Do not look for some great display of emotions. Sometimes there will be an emotional display and sometimes there will not be. We are saved by putting our faith in the finished work of Christ and not by emotions. People are coming to Christ, not simply agreeing with a presentation.

DRAW THE NET

After you have made the approach and have given the way of salvation, it is time to draw the net. At times, you may have the person bow his head and pray. When you pray, do not pray loudly. Perhaps you may wish to say when you are finished praying, "Now, if you will trust Christ as your Savior, I want you to take my hand." Let him know that it is not taking your hand that saves, but he is confessing to God that he is a lost sinner and expressing faith in Christ. The evidence of this is in reaching out to take your hand. We are saved by putting our faith in Jesus Christ to save us.

Determine in your heart that you are going to be more effective everywhere you go in telling lost people about the Lord Jesus Christ.

GIVE A WORD OF ENCOURAGEMENT

You may say, "I'm so happy that you have given your heart to the Lord today. I want to encourage you. I want your name and address so I can come by and visit with you, share some Bible verses with you, and help you get established in your new life as a Christian." Make arrangements to pick that person up and take him to church. Leave a tract. Leave with everything just as pleasant as you possibly can. If the person is someone you met in your travels, you may only be able to get the information necessary to send helpful materials and recommend a good church.

Determine in your heart that you are going to be more effective everywhere you go in telling lost people about the Lord Jesus Christ. In public places, seek to be used of God to win the lost. Some people will shake their heads at you and say, "No." But if you will be graciously persistent, you will see some people come to Christ and go to heaven. Determine in your heart that you are going to be a witness for Jesus Christ in public places. Every believer has a story to tell–TELL IT!

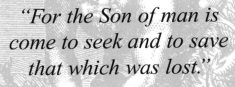

*"For the Son of man is
come to seek and to save
that which was lost."*

Luke 19:10

WITNESSING TO THOSE WHOM WE HAVE FAILED

any times in our Christian lives we know we have failed in the matter of witnessing. There was someone, some definite person to whom we should have witnessed and we walked out of the store, out of the home, out of the hospital room, or wherever it may have been, and we failed to witness to him. Perhaps it was someone we worked with for a while, and we did not witness to him. It may even be a family member we have failed to try to win to Christ. Now, here is the question—how can we go back and witness to people whom we have failed? I want to give you a few simple things that will help you and will also enable you to help others who have a deep sense of regret because they have failed to witness, sometimes even to loved ones.

WE MUST REALIZE IT IS OUR RESPONSIBILITY TO WITNESS TO ALL PEOPLE

You cannot give the gospel message to the wrong person. The unsaved must hear it, and the Christian will rejoice in it.

It is our responsibility in the home to witness to every family member. A man should do his first work for God in his home, seeking to win every family member to Christ.

As a Christian, you also have a responsibility to make sure that everyone who works around you on the job has heard the gospel. There will be a time to talk to each one. You are not paid to walk through the company with a Bible. The company is not paying you to preach; they are paying you to work. If you are on a break or lunch hour and can witness, or you notice there is a spare moment's time and you can give a testimony to people, then do that! Do not become a preacher on someone else's time when he is paying you to work. You will not gain a testimony—you will lose your testimony. If you get paid for an hour, do an hour's work. The opportunity will come for you to witness.

> *Do not become a preacher on someone else's time when he is paying you to work.*

Christian young people, who do not yet work, should get a burden for the students in their school classroom. They should witness to them, give them a gospel tract, share their testimony, and then personally go to them one by one and try to win them to Christ. It is our responsibility to witness to all people.

WE HAVE FAILED FELLOW WORKERS AND FRIENDS IN NOT WITNESSING TO THEM

Because we know we should witness to all people, we will realize at times that we have failed. We talk much about our fear of offending people when the real problem is not that we are afraid of offending people; we are afraid people are going to offend us! We have known some people for long periods of time and have never once told them how to know the Lord Jesus Christ as Savior.

ASK GOD TO FORGIVE YOU AND ASK THE PEOPLE TO FORGIVE YOU

Our hearts are stirred over our failure to witness to those around us. As we begin to wonder what can be done, we must first seek God's forgiveness. God will forgive (I John 1:9). Then we must seek the forgiveness of those whom we have failed. Simply go to the person you have failed and say, "I want you to forgive me." He will more than likely ask, "Well, what in the world for?" Say, "Because I am a Christian and I have never once told you how to know Christ. Will you please forgive me?" He will say, "Of course I'll forgive you." Then say, "Well, let me tell you how to know the Lord Jesus as your Savior."

How many of us know people we have failed in not trying to win them to Christ? Let us decide now that we are going to go right back to those people, ask them to forgive us, and seek to win them to the Savior. You may say, "Well, that's a little humbling to have to ask them to forgive me." Yes, it is; but we need to do it. It is hard to admit we are wrong and that we have failed, but we have. This will open many doors to witness to people.

WE MUST SEEK THE LOST

The Lord Jesus said that He came *"to seek and to save that which was lost"* (Luke 19:10). We need compassionate boldness to approach people about their relationship with God. People are everywhere. The problem does not lie in finding people, but in developing the best ways of gathering enough information about people to help them with their spiritual need.

DEVELOP WAYS OF GATHERING INFORMATION

When going to an area to visit, stop along the way and ask people for directions. After you have asked for directions, ask them, "Have you ever invited the Lord Jesus into your heart as your Savior?" When stopping to buy gas, ask the gas attendant if he is a Christian. Use every available means to talk to people and after you start the conversation, turn it to spiritual matters. Many can be won to Christ.

ORGANIZE A SYSTEM OF KEEPING NAMES

Carry something with you that allows you to record information you need on individuals. This becomes a record for further use. Take the time to write clearly so it will be readable when you look at it later.

GET NAMES AND ADDRESSES–LIST THE DATE, APPROXIMATE AGE, AND SPIRITUAL CONDITION

Specific information should be gathered when we talk to individuals about Christ. The information should include the correct name, address, age, and spiritual condition of the individuals.

Learn Abbreviations That Can Be Used for Spiritual Conditions (L-Lost, SNB-Saved Not Baptized)

If a person is lost, write an "L" above his name. If he has been saved but never baptized, put "SNB" by the name. This will help so very much when going back to deal with that particular individual.

This List Becomes a Prayer List

We cannot possibly win souls without prayer. To pray means to have God's power and His blessing in soul winning. Pray for the lost that you know, and pray earnestly for God to lead you to others who need the Savior. Also pray for God's help to be faithful to witness to those with whom you come into contact.

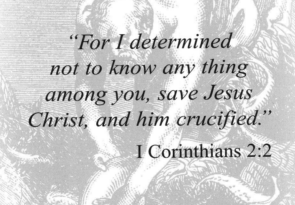

*"For I determined
not to know any thing
among you, save Jesus
Christ, and him crucified."*

I Corinthians 2:2

PRESENTING
THE GOSPEL

 e must follow the biblical method in leading the lost to Christ. The Lord Jesus Christ is the way of salvation, and we are to tell people of Him. Many are convicted when they do not witness. They know the Holy Spirit will help them. They also know that every Christian is a witness, but they are not leading the lost to Christ!

Soul winning is going in the power of the Holy Spirit, giving a clear presentation of the gospel, and bringing a person to the place of receiving or rejecting Jesus Christ. When presenting the gospel, we are to do three things. The *first* thing we must do is find out where people are spiritually. We can use the blueprint God has given us in Matthew 28:19-20 for a guideline to find out whether someone is saved, saved but never baptized, or saved and baptized but not attending a local, Bible-believing, Bible-preaching church. The *second* thing we are trying to do is present the gospel. The *third* thing to do is draw the net, meaning that once the gospel has been presented, we must bring the person to the place of receiving or rejecting Christ as personal Savior.

THE GOSPEL PRESENTATION

There are three things used in a gospel presentation.

Outline–This outline of the gospel involves a logical presentation of the gospel message. Always remember that every Christian has a story to tell. It is the story of coming to know the Lord Jesus Christ as Savior.

Scripture References–God's Word makes us *"wise unto salvation."* The Scriptures tell us the way to God through the Son of God, the Lord Jesus Christ.

Illustrations–Illustrations are stories, sometimes extended comments, that give understanding.

When I started witnessing, the only verse I could use was John 3:16. When you start out as a beginner in winning souls, the gospel presentation may be brief; but later it can be enlarged upon.

AN OUTLINE YOU CAN USE

I have put this outline into a gospel tract called, "Let Me Ask You This Question." The question is, "Do you know for sure if you died today you would go to heaven?" The outline follows the "logic of the gospel." This presents the way of salvation.

> Do you know for sure that if you died today you would go to heaven? Do you know the Lord Jesus Christ as your personal Savior? If Jesus Christ

returned today, do you know for sure that you would go to heaven with Him?

REALIZE THAT GOD LOVES YOU

God loves you and has a plan for your life.

"For God so loved the world, that he gave his only begotten Son, that whosoever believeth in him should not perish, but have everlasting life."

John 3:16

THE BIBLE SAYS THAT ALL MEN ARE SINNERS

Our God is holy and He declares that all men are sinners. Our sin separates us from God.

"For all have sinned, and come short of the glory of God."

Romans 3:23

God made man in His own image. He gave man the ability to choose right from wrong. We choose to sin. Our sins separate us from God.

GOD'S WORD ALSO SAYS THAT SIN MUST BE PAID FOR

"For the wages of sin is death..."   Romans 6:23

Wages means payment. The payment of our sin is death and hell, separation from God forever. If we continue in our sin, we shall die without Christ and be without God forever.

The Good News Is
That Christ Paid for Our Sins

All our sins were laid on Christ on the cross. He paid our sin debt for us. The Lord Jesus Christ died on the cross, and He rose from the dead. He is alive forevermore.

"But God commendeth his love toward us, in that, while we were yet sinners, Christ died for us." Romans 5:8

We Must Personally Pray and Receive Christ
by Faith as Our Savior

The Bible says, *"For whosoever shall call upon the name of the Lord shall be saved."* Romans 10:13

Pray and Receive Christ as Your Savior

Lord, I know that I am a sinner. If I died today, I would not go to heaven. Forgive my sin, come into my life and be my Savior. Help me live for You from this day forward. In Jesus' name, Amen.

The Bible says, *"For whosoever shall call upon the name of the Lord shall be saved."* Romans 10:13

New Life

Everlasting life begins when we receive Christ as our Savior.

Let Us Review

Realize That God Loves You..*John 3:16*

All Men Are Sinners..*Romans 3:23*

Sin Must Be Paid For..*Romans 6:23*

Christ Paid for Our Sins...*Romans 5:8*

We Must Personally Pray
and Receive Christ as Savior..................................*Romans 10:13*

We can use illustrations to help people understand. Remember that salvation is coming to know Christ. We are not simply making a presentation and getting an answer to our questions. We are telling people of the Lord Jesus Christ and His power to save. He has said, *"Him that cometh to me I will in no wise cast out"* (John 6:37).

When talking about God loving all people, sometimes I say, "Some people are harder to love than others, but God loves everyone. Do you know anyone who is hard to love?"

Sometimes, when I am explaining that by repentance and faith we must receive Christ as our Savior, I stand by a chair and say, "This chair can support me, but it does not until I trust it to do so. Christ can save you, but not until you put your faith in Him for salvation."

There are many easy ways to illustrate. Remember, when we are presenting the gospel we are doing three things: we are giving a logical outline, we are using Scripture references, and we are trying to use illustrations to help. You can talk a few minutes or an hour as you develop this way of telling the wonderful salvation story.

"Then they that gladly received his word were baptized: and the same day there were added unto them about three thousand souls."

Acts 2:41

CHAPTER TEN

LEADING CONVERTS TO OBEY CHRIST IN BELIEVER'S BAPTISM

he matter of obeying Christ in believer's baptism must be important to the soul winner. Often Christians who do soul-winning work say, "I am seeing people come to know Christ as Savior, but I am having trouble getting them to follow Him in baptism." I want to attempt to give those who desire to win souls some helpful ideas in this matter of leading converts to follow Christ in baptism.

OBEYING HIS COMMAND

The pattern for soul winning is given to us by the Lord Jesus. Read again and again Matthew 28:19-20. We are to go where the people are. We must then show them from God's Word how to be saved. We must lead them to follow Christ in baptism. Then we are to teach the new convert what Christ has commanded. It is such a simple plan to follow; do not try to complicate it. We are to be followers of the Lord Jesus Christ.

After salvation, the new Christian is to be obedient to Christ. The obedient Christian will follow the Lord Jesus in believer's baptism. We have the responsibility to teach this person what Christ has commanded Christians to do.

> *Baptism is a public declaration of faith in Christ by the believer before man. Not only does baptism show the death, burial, and resurrection of the Lord Jesus Christ, it also shows the believer's identification with Christ.*

The Lord Jesus Christ founded the New Testament church. In Matthew 16:18 He said, *"Upon this rock I will build my church."* The Bible also says in Ephesians 5:25, *"Christ also loved the church, and gave himself for it."* The church started with Christ and His disciples.

Christ gave to the church doctrines and ordinances. The doctrines of the church are its beliefs and teachings. The ordinances of a church are the things Christ said to observe. They are called ordinances because He commanded them or ordered them. In the New Testament church there are two ordinances; one is baptism, and the other is the Lord's Supper. Both ordinances of the church are beautiful pictures of spiritual truth. They have no saving power. They picture what the Lord Jesus has done for us.

The Lord's Supper was instituted by our Savior the night He was betrayed and delivered to die for our sins on the cross. No one is saved by partaking of the Lord's Supper. It is a memorial of the death of the Lord Jesus. We are to remember what He did for us on the cross.

Those who have trusted the Lord Jesus Christ as their Savior and followed Him in baptism may partake of the Lord's Supper.

Baptism is a burial and a resurrection. We are buried with Christ in the likeness of His death and raised in the likeness of His resurrection (Romans 6:1-4). Baptism is a public declaration of faith in Christ by the believer before man. Not only does baptism show the death, burial, and resurrection of the Lord Jesus Christ, it also shows the believer's identification with Christ. Baptism is his full declaration of his own death in Christ (II Corinthians 5:14): dead to sin, dead to self, and dead to the old life. It is also his declaration of being raised with Christ, after burying the old life, to walk in newness of life with Him.

Teach the new convert that baptism is only for believers. A person must be saved before he can be baptized. The Lord Jesus said that after a person is saved, he is to be baptized (Matthew 28:19-20).

Explain to the new Christian that the Bible teaches baptism by immersion. This means going under the water and coming up out of the water. As the believer stands in the water, the water crossses his body like the cross where the Lord Jesus died. Going beneath the water is a picture of how the Lord Jesus went into the grave. Coming up out of the water is a picture of how the Lord Jesus came out of the grave alive forever.

WHEN A PERSON HAS TRUSTED CHRIST AS SAVIOR:

Show him Bible verses on the assurance of salvation: John 10:27-29, John 3:16, Romans 8:35, 38-39.

Ask him, "Do you believe God's Word?"

Ask, "Are you thankful for what God has done for you?"

Say, "Then you should be willing to obey the Lord." Turn to Matthew 28:19-20 and show him exactly what God's Word says he should do.

Out of a grateful heart, in obedience to Christ, the new believer should be baptized.

Be sure you have his name, address, and phone number.

Make arrangements to get this new believer to church.

Take very special care of him when he comes to church that first time.

Sit with him in the service.

Explain that the pastor is going to preach and then invite him and others like him to profess their faith in Christ.

The new Christian should be able to express the basic idea about what has taken place in his life.

Assure him he will not have to make a long speech. Tell him what he will be asked. Relieve his fears.

Introduce him to the pastor or personal worker and explain what has taken place in the person's life.

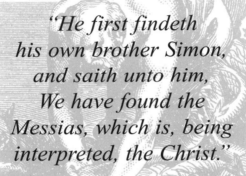

*"He first findeth
his own brother Simon,
and saith unto him,
We have found the
Messias, which is, being
interpreted, the Christ."*

John 1:41

TEACHING NEW BELIEVERS TO FOLLOW CHRIST

 oul winners have a responsibility to those they win to the Lord. In one way they become the spiritual parents to these babes in Christ. It would be even more correct to say that it is the local church that has a responsibility to these new Christians and the personal soul winner becomes the extension of his church to those he leads to Christ.

Our responsibility is to help every new Christian grow in the Lord and become faithfully involved in a local, Bible-believing, Bible-preaching church. Every new Christian should follow Christ in baptism, attend church faithfully, read his Bible, pray, seek to win others to Christ, and tithe. We are to make disciples. This is more than a "follow-up" program; it is teaching the new Christian to follow Christ.

The Responsibility of the Church to the New Believer

Believers need to be taught the things that are essential to living a victorious Christian life. This is the responsibility of the church. The new believer needs to know:

What the Word of God declares about the *assurance of salvation.*

How to have *victory over sin* in the daily life.

The fact that *God loves* him and will *forgive* and cleanse all sins.

How to *read the Bible* and *apply it to life.*

The *necessity of prayer* and *how to pray.*

The place and importance of *the local church in the work of God* in the world today.

How to *share the gospel with the lost.*

What the New Christian Does for the Local Church

New Christians do certain things for a local church that no other group can do.

New converts usually come from groups of people who are not being reached by the ministry of the church; therefore, their friendships and families *open up new avenues of evangelistic outreach and ministry.*

New converts have excitement in their new Christian lives which *breeds a contagious enthusiasm among others in the church.*

New converts express a strong *loyalty to the church* and are eager to support and participate in the ministry of the local church. New converts have a *glowing testimony and exemplify a dynamic zeal* in telling others what Christ has done for them.

THINGS TO REMEMBER WHEN DEALING WITH NEW CONVERTS

Remember that these are "babes in Christ." They are newborns and they must be treated with special care. We must remember certain things when dealing with these new Christians in order for them to grow and develop.

Like all babes, *they must receive proper love and attention.* We must begin immediately to instruct them in the things of God and show them how to live the Christian life.

They must receive the proper feeding. This feeding comes from the Word of God. The diet must, of course, begin with the milk of the Word and then progress to the meat.

We must not expect these new babes in Christ to have "instant maturity." We will encounter some problems in growth along the way.

The Great Commission is obeyed when the "evangelized" become "evangelists," when the new Christians are telling others how to be saved.

When properly cared for, new converts will grow into mature Christians who will reach others with the gospel. The Great Commission is obeyed when the "evangelized" become "evangelists," when the new Christians are telling others how to be saved.

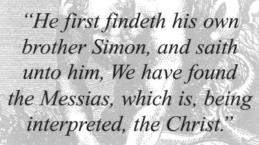

*"He first findeth his own
brother Simon, and saith
unto him, We have found
the Messias, which is, being
interpreted, the Christ."*

John 1:41

WON BY ONE

hink how truly wonderful it is to be used of God to speak with people about the Lord Jesus Christ and win them to Him. Years ago, a Christian businessman by the name of Art DeMoss encouraged me to develop a simple presentation for training Christians to win the lost to Christ. This chapter provides those things that can be used in bringing people to the Lord Jesus.

The Bible says in John 1:42, *"And he brought him to Jesus."* Two men who had been disciples of John the Baptist started following the Lord Jesus. They abode with Him that day and trusted Him as their personal Savior. One of the men who followed the Lord Jesus was Andrew, Simon Peter's brother, and the Bible says, *"He first findeth his own brother, Simon, . . . and he brought him to Jesus."* We do not know exactly where Andrew found Peter, perhaps along the seaside or on a path going to the seaside, maybe close to home, but he found him. When he found him, he was thrilled because he had trusted the Lord Jesus as his personal Savior. The Bible says he brought Peter to Jesus Christ. Peter was "won by one." The one that won him to Christ was his own brother, Andrew. Those of us who know Christ as our Savior have a message that lost men must hear. They must believe it and receive it. God has entrusted us with the sacred responsibility of bringing the lost to Christ.

This is not simply another attempt at giving a lesson on soul winning. I want us to bring together everything discussed in this book. May God stir us, help us, and equip us to win the lost to Christ.

PREPARATION

KNOW FOR SURE THAT YOU HAVE ETERNAL LIFE

The foundational principle for soul winning is found in Matthew 16:13-16, *"When Jesus came into the coasts of Caesarea Philippi, he asked his disciples, saying, Whom do men say that I the Son of man am?"* When the people recognized the authority of the Lord Jesus as He spoke, they thought He must be John the Baptist. When they saw the miracles that the Lord Jesus performed, they said He was Elijah. Others beheld the tears and compassion of the Lord Jesus and said He was Jeremiah. Christ stopped His disciples and asked them, *"But whom say ye that I am?"* And Peter, the spokesman for the group, said, *"Thou art the Christ, the Son of the living God."* If you know that Jesus Christ is God's Son and that He has changed your life and can change others, you are ready to tell people about Him.

The first time I ever had the opportunity to lead someone to Christ, I was still a teenager. I went soul winning with a man in our church. I had not planned to do any witnessing. I was only to be the silent partner. I was going to sit by and let my friend do all the talking. We went to a home to see a certain man, but when we arrived at the home, the man was not there. I thought we were going to leave, but my partner said to the lady of the house, "Are you a Christian?" She said, "Yes." Then he asked the teenage boy standing by his mother's side if he were a Christian and the teenager said he was not. The soul winner was determined to tell the boy how to be saved. After gaining permission from the mother to speak to her son, we went into the house, sat down, and started talking. Right in the middle of his conversation, the man of the house arrived. Unexpectedly, my friend turned to me and said, "Clarence, you talk to the boy; I'm going to talk to his father." The young man and I walked out of the house into the yard, and my friend and the father stayed inside.

If you know that Jesus Christ is God's Son and know He has changed your life and can change others, you are ready to tell people about Him.

The teenage boy leaned up against the side of his ranch-style house and waited for me to speak. I did not know what to do. I knew I had been saved and I could share a little bit of my testimony, so I said to this fellow, "Salvation is like a gift. The package is wrapped up, the bow is tied, and God will give it to you. It's the Lord Jesus, and if you will take Him as your Savior, He will come to live in you. Will you trust Him?" It was a fumbling attempt, but he said, "Yes, I will." He asked God to forgive his sin and save him. When I got through, I thought, "If the Lord can use me, He can use anyone." God did something in my heart that day, and I thank Him for it. I truly realized that *"salvation is of the Lord"* and the Lord will use us to tell the story.

KNOW THE WAY OF SALVATION AND CARRY A NEW TESTAMENT

Anyone who knows the Lord Jesus can tell others. We must know how to be saved in order to tell others of Him.

Carry a New Testament and gospel tracts. You must be able to give God's Word. At times you may only be able to quote the Scriptures; therefore, work to memorize verses that explain the way of salvation.

GIVE ATTENTION TO YOUR APPEARANCE

Make sure your hair and clothing are right. Ladies should dress like ladies, and men should dress like men. Look your best because you are an ambassador for Jesus Christ.

REALIZATION

REALIZE MEN ARE LOST ALL ABOUT US

Be conscious of the lost people around you each day. Pray and seek the filling of God's Spirit. As a believer, you are indwelt by the Holy Spirit, so yield your life to Him for His filling. We are His witnesses.

Remember the two types of personal evangelism mentioned earlier–"contact" evangelism and "planned" evangelism. We must learn in our contacts with people each day how to turn the conversation to spiritual things and present the gospel.

I went into an old-fashioned drugstore a number of years ago, sat down to get a sandwich, and a fellow sat down beside me. I turned to him and said, "Excuse me. Let me ask you this question, are you a Christian?" He did not answer. I said again, "Excuse me (a little louder), are you a Christian? Have you received Christ into your heart?" He noticed that I was talking to him, so he took some napkins from the napkin holder in front of him and wrote in big letters, "I AM DEAF." I reached into the napkin holder and took a big handful of napkins, and wrote on one, "Are you a Christian?" and handed it to him. He reached inside the napkin holder, took a big handful and began to write, and this is what he wrote, "I grew up in Texas. I lived twenty years of my life, and not one time did anyone ever ask me if I were a Christian." And in big, bold letters he wrote, "I AM AN ATHEIST. DON'T BOTHER ME."

I thought that if someone who had come in contact with him when his heart was young and searching had simply taken the time to give him the gospel, he could be going to heaven today instead of going to hell. People are all around us; they are everywhere. Do not think that they will not hear because many of them are waiting to hear. Be soul-conscious. You cannot witness to the wrong person.

> *Because I know Christ, I owe the Christian message to others. I am indebted because someone told me.*

SOMEONE TOLD YOU ABOUT THE SAVIOR

Remember, someone told you how to be saved. When the Lord Jesus stood before His disciples and said, *"Go ye into all the world and preach the gospel,"* that is exactly what they did. They told people the way of salvation through Jesus Christ, and when those people got saved, they told others. When those people got saved, they told others. Winding through the centuries, the gospel found its way one day to a man who told me. If I do not tell others, they will not hear. Because I know Christ, I owe the Christian message to others. I am indebted because someone told me.

MEN WITHOUT CHRIST ARE LOST AND GOING TO HELL

Realize that men without Christ are lost and going to hell, a real hell! A Christless life ends in a Christless eternity. Let that thought grip your soul. The story in Luke 16:22-24 says,

> *And it came to pass, that the beggar died, and was carried by the angels into Abraham's bosom: the rich man also died, and was buried; and in hell he lifted up his eyes, being in torments, and seeth Abraham afar off, and Lazarus in his bosom. And he cried and said, Father Abraham, have mercy on me, and send Lazarus, that he may dip the tip of his finger in water, and cool my tongue; for I am tormented in this flame.*

CHRIST CAN AND WILL SAVE

It is encouraging to know that no one is so lost, so hell-bound, so wretched, so blinded by sin that Christ cannot save him. You are never going to meet anyone that the Lord cannot save if that person will seek forgiveness of his sin and trust Christ. What a glorious thought! If it is a businessman who makes over a hundred thousand a year, or if it is a poor man on welfare, it makes no difference; the Lord Jesus can save anyone! There is no harlot walking the streets of the city that Christ cannot save. There is no drunkard lying in an alley that Christ cannot save. All people need to be saved.

GOD WILL USE YOU TO WIN SOULS

You will never do anything any greater in your life than win someone to Jesus Christ. God wants to use you. Our wonderful Lord has chosen to use men to tell the gospel story.

Visitation

Go With a Purpose

Promise God that you will go after souls. Obligate yourself to God to go. The best thing to do is to say, "Lord, I promise You, I will go after souls." This is where the emphasis needs to be placed. Go with the purpose to win souls. We do not go just to knock on a few doors in order to say, "Well, I've fulfilled my responsibility. I've done enough. I went visiting." No! We are going with a purpose to win people to Christ. We can win the lost if we simply go after souls. Go with a purpose; that purpose is to win the lost to Christ.

We are going with a purpose to win people to Christ.

Many years ago, a little girl went to a Sunday School class one Sunday morning and her teacher said, "Next Sunday I want us to do something different. I do not want you to come alone to class next week. I want you to bring a friend; and every person who brings a friend will get a star by her name on the class roll." The little girl sat there that morning and in her heart she dreamed of seeing a star by her name the next Sunday morning. She was going to do all she could to bring a friend to Sunday School. As soon as Sunday School was over, she started to ask people to attend class with her the next week; but no one would agree. As the week passed, no promises came. Finally, as Sunday neared, she thought, "There's one person who will go with me, and that's my daddy." She knew she could get Daddy to come. Her daddy's name was Stephen Paxson. He was an unusual man. He had a limp and a stutter and played a fiddle in a square dance group on Saturday nights, but he loved his little girl. When she asked, "Daddy, will you go?" he said, "Yes, I'll go." Sunday morning came, and the little girl walked back into the little girls' class with her daddy by her side. When the teacher saw Daddy there, she knew that something was different, and she needed to lay aside the normal lesson of the Sunday School and simply give the gospel message. As she did, God blessed; and when the lesson was concluded, Stephen Paxson, a stuttering, limping fiddle player asked the Lord Jesus to save him.

The story does not end there. Stephen Paxson said, "That's not enough. I want a purpose for my life." He gave up playing the fiddle in the square dance group on Saturday nights, bought an old horse and started traveling and starting Sunday Schools like the one in which he heard the gospel. Before Stephen Paxson died, he rode over 100,000 miles on horseback. He started 1,314 Sunday Schools, and he personally led 83,000 boys and girls to Jesus Christ.

GO TWO BY TWO

The Lord Jesus sent people out two by two. One person should do the talking while the other serves as the silent prayer partner. The silent partner clears the way for the soul winner to witness and earnestly prays while his partner shares the gospel. Going two by two also helps to avoid the appearance of evil and gives support to the soul winner.

CONFRONTATION

There was a certain man in the city of Boston over a hundred years ago who taught a Sunday School class of young men, and he was burdened about all of them knowing Christ as their personal Savior. The man's name was Edward Kimball. He was a rather timid man, and even though he taught a class, he did not really have a good feeling about addressing people one on one; but he got a burden for his class members and wanted all of them to be saved.

One of the young men in his class worked at a shoe store in Boston, so Mr. Kimball started down to the shoe store one day to see him. He reached the shoe store, and he was so nervous and afraid that he walked right by it. He came under deep conviction, turned around, and entered the store.

When Mr. Kimball went in, the fellow he went to see was not working out front; he was back in the stock room putting up shoes. Kimball walked to the young man's side and as best he could, in a nervous kind of way, gave him the gospel message. To Mr. Kimball's surprise, the young fellow, right there in the storeroom, bowed his head, asked God to forgive him of his sin, and trusted the Lord Jesus Christ as his Savior.

One person should do the talking while the other serves as the silent prayer partner.

Edward Kimball later died and went to glory. Nobody much remembers him; but the young man that he confronted that day in the shoe store was named D. L. Moody. Moody became one of the most renown evangelists of all time.

BEGIN THE CONVERSATION CASUALLY

Recall how the Lord Jesus confronted the woman at the well. The Lord Jesus began by speaking to this woman about a very normal topic of conversation. Then, He turned the conversation to spiritual things telling her of His power to give eternal life. He made her aware of her spiritual need, and she trusted Him as her Savior.

DISCERN THE TRUE SPIRITUAL CONDITION OF THE PERSON

Do not begin by giving him the gospel right away. The person may already be a Christian. Find out where he is spiritually before you get started. God has given us a blueprint to follow in Matthew 28:19-20.

PEOPLE MUST HEAR THE GOSPEL

There is no Good News until there is bad news. The bad news is that we are sinners and our sin separates us from God. Believe that people want to hear. When you meet someone, say, "Let me ask you this question," and ask him if he has ever trusted Christ. If the answer comes back, "No," just simply say, "Allow me to show you from the Bible how to know the Lord Jesus Christ as your Savior." Take your New Testament and open it while you are making this statement. If the answer is yes, then ask the person to tell you about it. The person who has trusted Christ as Savior will be glad to tell you how he came to Christ.

STAY ON THE SUBJECT OF SALVATION

The Devil will try to sidetrack you. Some people will say things like, "Well, now, wait a minute. Is it wrong to smoke cigarettes?" "I do not have to go to church every Sunday to be a Christian." "You know, different people believe different things about the Bible." Do not be distracted from your mission. Your mission is to tell the truth of God's Word concerning the gospel.

STAY WITH THE BIBLE

Do not confuse people by going all through the Bible from book to book. Give clear, strong verses from God's Word.

SHOW HIM THAT HE IS A SINNER–REFER TO YOURSELF AS A SINNER

When you use the verse to show someone that he is a sinner, state first that you are a sinner. Simply say, "We're all sinners. I am a sinner, you are a sinner, we are all sinners."

SHOW HIM THE WAGES OF SIN

When I read Romans 6:23, *"For the wages of sin is death,"* I say, "Wages means payment. You work, you get wages. That's the pay you get. The payment of sin is death. That is death and hell, separation from God forever."

EXPLAIN TO HIM THAT JESUS CHRIST PAID OUR SIN DEBT

This is an excellent place to use an illustration about Christ bearing our sins on the cross. Our sins were put on Him. He paid our debt so that we would not have to pay it.

REVIEW THE MAIN POINTS—BE SURE HE UNDERSTANDS

Be as clear as possible presenting the truth from God's Word and trust the Holy Spirit to give understanding.

SHOW HIM THAT HE MUST RECEIVE CHRIST BY FAITH

Romans 10:13 is a good verse to use here, *"For whosoever shall call upon the name of the Lord shall be saved."* Sometimes I stand by a chair and say, "This chair can support me, but it doesn't until I trust it to do so. Christ can save you, but not until you put your faith in Him for salvation."

STATE, "LET'S HAVE PRAYER."

Be sure the lost person understands what you have said. Encourage the person to pray, asking God for forgiveness of sin and trusting the Lord Jesus Christ as his personal Savior.

Invitation

As the Lord by His Spirit has convicted the lost person of his sin, lead that person to pray and seek God's forgiveness of sin and by faith trust the Lord Jesus Christ as Savior. The Bible says in Romans 10:13, *"For whosoever shall call upon the name of the Lord shall be saved."* This is God's promise. Put your faith in God's Word. God will keep His Word.

Explanation

Explain God's Promise to Save

Tell him what the Bible has promised. This individual has made the most important decision of his life. Salvation is a decision and a revelation. Of course, the lost person of his own will must place his faith in Christ for salvation. But be assured that God's Word is true. Our Lord said, *"Him that cometh to me I will in no wise cast out"* (John 6:37). Christ will make Himself known to those who call upon Him for salvation.

Give Him Verses of Assurance

John 3:16 is a great verse on assurance. Give the new believer the truth of God's Word on this matter. You may wish to read Romans 8:38-39 or John 10:27-29 to the new believer. Before you attempt to get him to obey Christ as a new Christian, lead him to see the promise God has made to keep him saved forever. He has *eternal* life in Christ.

MANIFESTATION

PRAY A PRAYER OF THANKSGIVING

Instruct the new Christian to thank the Lord for his salvation.

LEAD HIM TO MAKE
A PUBLIC PROFESSION OF FAITH

This is where we go right back to God's blueprint in Matthew 28:19-20. Take your Bible and go over it. Read to him Matthew 28:19-20 and show him that Christ commanded us to go to sinners. Show him that we are to teach people how to be saved. Show him the next thing God says to do is to follow Christ in baptism and then lead him to see that we are to be taught the Word of God after we are saved.

Go by and get him for the next church service. Relieve his fears by letting him know that you plan to sit with him during the church service and go with him to speak with the pastor or personal worker during the invitation. Do not forget the responsibility we have to follow up these new babes in Christ. Plan to have fellowship with him in the days ahead and lead him to follow Christ. Begin immediately to get him into God's Word and instruct him to follow the Lord Jesus Christ.

"And the things that thou hast heard of me among many witnesses, the same commit thou to faithful men, who shall be able to teach others also."

II Timothy 2:2

CHAPTER THIRTEEN

TEACHING
OTHERS ALSO

 he book of II Timothy is the farewell given by the apostle Paul. There are twenty-nine different people mentioned by name in this book of the Bible. The thought of these people reminds us that God does His work through people. It is our responsibility to not only win the lost, but also to teach others the things that have been committed to us. Every witness needs to be training another to witness.

The Bible says in II Timothy 2:1-4,

> *Thou therefore, my son, be strong in the grace that is in Christ Jesus. And the things that thou hast heard of me among many witnesses, the same commit thou to faithful men, who shall be able to teach others also. Thou therefore endure hardness, as a good soldier of Jesus Christ. No man that warreth*

entangleth himself with the affairs of this life; that he may please him who hath chosen him to be a soldier.

Note the expression in verse two, *"...able to teach others also."* Our Lord has given us only one way to train others to do His work. He taught us by His example.

> The way we approach this subject of laborers reveals what we believe about God.

The Lord Jesus said to His disciples in Matthew 9:38, *"Pray ye therefore the Lord of the harvest, that he will send forth labourers into his harvest."* The way to get laborers is not to recruit laborers; the way to get laborers is to pray the Lord of the harvest that He would send forth laborers into His harvest.

The way we approach this subject of laborers reveals what we believe about God. We either believe the work depends upon us or upon the Lord. Of course, there is the human element; the Lord uses human instrumentality. But God says we are to pray to the Lord of the harvest that He would send forth laborers into the harvest.

If you are laboring, someone has prayed for you. Someone prayed that God would raise up a laborer. You are an answer to someone's prayer. We must pray for laborers.

When God gives laborers, He tells us what we are to do. The Word of God says very clearly, *"And the things that thou hast heard of me among many witnesses, the same commit thou to faithful men, who shall be able to teach others also."*

We find here the apostle Paul speaking to Timothy. Paul was at least thirty years older than Timothy. Notice in this verse that the Bible talks about Paul, Timothy, faithful men, and others. Paul taught Timothy; Timothy was to teach faithful men; faithful men were to teach others. The work of personal evangelism must be taught to others.

You may not be a pastor, but if you are a Christian and you are a laborer for the Lord, it is your responsibility to do your best with God's help to teach someone else who will be able to teach others also. If you teach a Sunday School class, you should challenge the students to teach the lesson to others throughout the week. All those who hear and receive the truth are accountable to teach others also.

I say often that, when God allowed me to meet and marry my wife, the most wonderful thing God did for me was to give me two sons. I am to impart to those boys what God had imparted to me. I do not believe it is my responsibility to try to train everyone else in the world and neglect my own children. Of course, no one ever does everything he should do, but God gives us a responsibility in the family to entrust certain things to our family members.

> *If you are laboring, someone has prayed for you. Someone prayed that God would raise up a laborer.*

When we examine God's work, we find this same thing to be true. There is always the hand print of a human being on another human being. Have you invested your life in the life of someone else?

THERE IS A PRINCIPLE THAT MUST BE FOLLOWED

Think of how many marvelous things could be accomplished if all of us took to heart the responsibility to teach others also. You may say, "I don't know much." It does not make any difference how much you know. If you know the Lord, start by telling someone about Jesus Christ.

Consider what the Bible says in Luke chapter five. The Lord Jesus was walking by the seaside early in the morning. Peter and the rest of the fishermen had been out all night and had caught nothing. The Lord Jesus told Peter to cast his nets. Peter took his boat back into the waters and cast a net, and they caught a great catch of fish.

Peter looked back to the silhouette of the Son of God on the shore. Then he went back and fell at the feet of the Lord Jesus. In Luke 5:8-11 the Bible says,

> *When Simon Peter saw it, he fell down at Jesus' knees, saying, Depart from me; for I am a sinful man, O Lord. For he was astonished, and all that were with him, at the draught of the fishes which they had taken: and so was also James, and John, the sons of Zebedee, which were partners with Simon. And Jesus said unto Simon, Fear not; from henceforth thou shalt catch men. And when they had brought their ships to land, they forsook all, and followed him.*

They followed the Lord Jesus. Christ called disciples, learners who could be taught. He established here a principle for us to follow.

In Matthew 11:28-30 the Bible says, *"Come unto me, all ye that labour and are heavy laden, and I will give you rest. Take my yoke upon you, and learn of me; for I am meek and lowly in heart: and ye shall find rest unto your souls. For my yoke is easy, and my burden is light."*

The Lord says, "Get in this yoke with Me. Understand what I am doing." This gives us the picture of a double yoke with the oxen in the yoke side by side. The Lord says, "I'm on one side, you get on the other side and learn of Me." There is a principle that we are to teach others also.

People have invested their lives in me, and I want to invest my life in others. Someone reached people for Christ and those people reached others and those people reached others and finally, through the centuries, someone reached me. And I am going to do all I can to reach others. This principle is clearly taught in the Word of God.

The apostle Paul was teaching Timothy just as Jesus Christ had taught His disciples. Paul was leaving this farewell address to Timothy, "Timothy, this is the way God's work is to be done."

Women, find a young woman that you can encourage and help in the Lord. Men, find a man and invest your life in him. Older couples, find a young couple and invest your life in them. This is the way God intends for His work to be done.

We must pass on to someone else the things we have learned. This is the principle we find in the Word of God. Those who know must tell those who do not know. I was taught to lead the lost to Christ by an elderly man in our church when I was only eighteen years old. I became his Timothy in the matter of soul winning.

THERE IS A PRICE TO PAY

Second, there is a price to pay. Consider what the Bible says in II Timothy 2:3, *"Thou therefore endure hardness, as a good soldier of Jesus Christ."*

The Bible says we are to endure hardness. Our ability or inability to help others as Christians is related entirely to the private, secret preparation we make as Christians. The character of our Christian life is determined by the time we spend with the Lord Jesus. We cannot be a help to others unless we are walking with God.

What people truly need most is not a lecture in a classroom; they need to see a holy life standing before them. May God help us to drive this home, not simply to the heart of the person we hope to teach, but may it be driven home to our own hearts. We must take the time to be holy people.

There is a price to pay. *"Study to shew thyself approved unto God, a workman that needeth not to be ashamed, rightly dividing the word of truth"* (II Timothy 2:15). Time and prayer is a price to pay. Digging deep wells of Scripture knowledge is a price to pay.

We must remain vigilant in our personal lives if we are going to be able to teach other people. The note we sound must be clear if we are going to teach other people. The way we state truths should be as close as possible to the very words of Scripture if we are going to teach other people.

There is price to pay for holy living. It is time alone with God. There is a price to pay in passing the truth on to other people, pouring out your life into others. It takes something from you.

Would it be better for us to try to leave our children great wealth or a godly heritage? We know the answer to that question. This demands a price that has to be paid. On a daily basis, we must be the Christians God desires for us to be.

THERE IS A PERSON TO PLEASE

The Bible says in II Timothy 2:4, *"...that he may please him who hath chosen him to be a soldier."* Who has chosen us to be soldiers? The answer to that question is the Lord Jesus. He is the One we are to please.

There are many things that people know how to do that they never teach anyone else to do. I know a young man who is a builder who repairs and reconstructs old things that have been hand carved. Someone taught him how to do that. But if he does not teach someone else, that craft will cease to exist.

What has happened in the ministry and in Christian homes is that Christians have ceased to teach the next generation what God has taught us in His Word. We have left the instruction to people who do not walk with God and who have found a wordly way to try to do God's work. This is our fault because God has told us exactly how it should be done.

If we are going to be able to teach others also, there is a principle to be followed, a price to pay, and a person to please.

Ladies, turn your eyes back to the Lord Jesus and what He has given you to do. Men, fix your eyes back on the Lord and what He has given you to do.

What God has given us to do is to leave behind faithful people who have been trained to teach others also. This is the way God's work is to be done.

Win souls and take someone with you that you are teaching to win souls. The soul winner you train will be able to teach others.

As I look back, I realize I have received a great heritage. I am grateful for it. As I look forward, I should see that I have invested my life in teaching others also.

Take responsibility, not only to witness to the lost, but also to teach someone else how to witness to the lost. Take the things you have learned and teach them to someone else.

ABOUT THE AUTHOR

Clarence Sexton is the pastor of the Temple Baptist Church and founder of Crown College in Knoxville, Tennessee. He has written more than twenty books and booklets. He speaks in conferences throughout the United States and has conducted training sessions for pastors and Christian workers in several countries around the world. He and his wife, Evelyn, have been married for thirty-five years. They have two grown sons and six grandchildren. For more information about the ministry of Clarence Sexton, visit our website at www.FaithfortheFamily.com.

OTHER HELPFUL BOOKS BY CLARENCE SEXTON:

THE LORD IS MY SHEPHERD

EARNESTLY CONTEND
FOR THE FAITH

THE CHRISTIAN HOME

TRUTHS EVERY
CHRISTIAN NEEDS
TO KNOW

LORD, SEND A
REVIVAL

THE PARABLES
OF JESUS

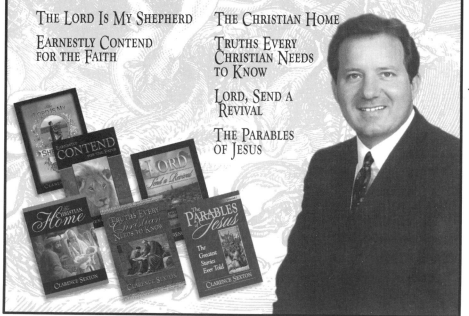